The Human Face of Jesus

Meditation and Commentary on the Gospel of Luke

D0862173

The Human Face of Jesus

Meditation and Commentary on the Gospel of Luke

Alfred McBride, O. Praem.

Our Sunday Visitor Publishing Division
Our Sunday Visitor, Inc.
Huntington, Indiana 46750

Nihil Obstat: Reverend Richard J. Murphy, O.M.I.
               Censor Deputatus

Imprimatur: Reverend Msgr. William J. Kane, V.G.
               Vicar General for the Archdiocese of Washington
               July 16, 1991

The nihil obstat and imprimatur are official declarations that a book
or pamphlet is free of doctrinal or moral error. No implication is contained therein that those who have granted the nihil obstat and the imprimatur agree with the content, opinions, or statements expressed.

ISBN: 0-87973-358-6
LCCCN: 91-62164

PRINTED IN THE UNITED STATES OF AMERICA

Cover design by Rebecca J. Heaston
Editorial production by Kelley L. Renz
358

Dedicated to these priest friends who have been pillars of companionship, faith and inspiration to me: Jack Meyers, Jim Hawker, Frank Kelly, Neil Heery, John Bradley, John Forliti, Leo Farley, Paul Mahan, Mike Foley, John Foley, Tommy Oates, Mike Carroll, Frank Barrett, Jack Murphy, Gery Meehan, Roman Vanasse, Louie Freiberg, Joe Serano, Andrew Ciferni, and Bob Cornell.

Contents

Foreword

On the road to Emmaus, Jesus gave his two friends a Scripture lesson. He took the Bible as though it were a loaf of bread and broke it open to feed their hearts, minds, feelings, and souls. He explained how the prophets, wisdom speakers, psalm singers, storytellers, and patriarchs sang and spoke of the essential link between the sufferings of the messiah and his glory. "Was it not necessary that the Messiah should suffer these things and so enter his glory?" (Lk. 24:6).

Luke does not give us the details of that remarkable Scripture lesson, other than to say the listeners were so moved that their hearts burned within them. Jesus gave them an experience of Scripture that caused a personal spiritual and moral conversion. The Christian interpretation of Scripture ever since has drawn two essential guidelines from that scene. First, all of Scripture illumines the meaning and purpose of Jesus Christ's work of salvation. Second, the biblical words call each of us to a faith conversion to Jesus Christ.

No interpreter of Scripture ever understood these principles better than St. Augustine. For him the soul was the home of all the feelings in the body. Since Christians were members of Christ's Body, they could get in touch with the inner life of Jesus, his soul if you will. As Augustine scanned the pages of Scripture, he found in the psalms the record of the feelings of Jesus. The psalms and the gospels were more than two books written in different periods of history, they were the seamless garment of the love story between God and people, one text illuminating the other.

The Christ of Augustine's sermons on the gospels possesses the quiet majesty of classic art. But in his commentaries on the psalms, Augustine comes upon a flood of emotions and applies them to Jesus. The figure of the passionate King David supplies the vision of the emotions of Jesus. Hence it is Christ's voice that is heard in the psalms, "a voice singing happily, a voice rejoicing in hope, a voice sighing in its present state. We should know his voice, feel it intimately, make it our own" (*Commentary on Psalms*, 42,1).

At the same time, Augustine wanted to do more than stir up feeling in the listeners to his Scripture sermons. He wanted to break bread and feed the multitude. As a boy, he had stolen fruit to share with his comrades. As a bishop, he raided the fields of Scripture to feed his parishioners to whom he ministered for forty years. "I go to feed so I can give you to eat. I lay before you that from which I draw my life" (*Fragments*, 2,4). He was interested in converting his listeners to Jesus ever more deeply through the Scriptures.

He wrote to Jerome that he could never be a disinterested Bible scholar. "If I gain any new knowledge of Scripture, I pay it out immediately to God's people" (*Letter*, 73,2).

Pope John Paul II stressed these same principles about Scripture interpretation in an address to the members of the Biblical Commission. He noted with satisfaction the progress being made in modern Catholic biblical scholarship since the encyclical *Providentissimus* written by Pope Leo XIII in 1893. He cited the many forms of scientific analysis of Scripture which have developed, such as the study of literary forms, semiotics, and narrative analysis.

He dwelt on the "limitations" of the new methods and asked his listeners to avoid the excesses of the swings of fashion in Scripture interpretation, for example, one school totally preoccupied with history and another one forgetting history altogether. He also advised his audience to observe the one-sidedness of some interpreters of Scripture such as those who cite Vatican II's document on Scripture (*Dei Verbum*) in support of the use of scientific methods, but seem to forget the other teaching of the council that interpreters should never forget the divine authorship of the Bible.

His next words deserve to be quoted in full:

The Bible has certainly been written in human language. Its interpretation requires the methodical use of the science of language. But it is also God's Word. Exegesis (Scripture interpretation) would be seriously incomplete if it did not shed light on the theological significance of Scripture.

We must not forget that Christian exegesis is a theological discipline, a deepening of the faith. This entails an interior tension between historical research founded on verifiable facts and research in the spiritual order based on faith in Christ. There is a great temptation to eliminate this inner tension by renouncing one or another of these two orientations ... to be content with a subjective interpretation which is wrongly called "spiritual," or a scientific interpretation which makes the texts "sterile"

—English Edition of *L'Osservatore Romano*, April 22, 1991

This commentary/meditation which you are about to read was written with this total vision in mind. You will not find it heavily scientific because it was not meant to be a popularization of the scientific methods of interpretation. At the same time, it is meant to reflect the beneficial results of scientific studies. You will discover it is aimed at opening up the person, message, and work of Jesus Christ whose work of salvation in union with the Father and the Holy Spirit is presented. Therefore, Jesus centered and faith growth envisioned.

It is my hope that these reflections will draw you to love the Bible, and in so doing, love Christ, yourself, and others. We are thus loving more than a book or sacred texts, we are in a total love affair. Perhaps Chaim Potok's description of the "Dance of the Torah" has something to say to us here. The scene is a Hasidic Synagogue in the Williamsburg section of Brooklyn. A religious festival is in progress and the participants have reached a part of the ceremony where scrolls of the Torah are passed around and certain privileged members are allowed to dance with it. We pick up the scene as the principal character, who has been agonizing about his faith and its relation to life, is handed the scroll.

> I held the scroll as something precious to me, a living being with whose soul I was forever bound, this Sacred Scroll, this Word, this Fire of God, this Source for my own creation, this velvet encased Fountain of All Life which I now clasped in a passionate embrace. I danced with the Torah for a long time, following the line of dancers through the steamy air of the synagogue and out into the chill tumultuous street and back into the synagogue and then reluctantly yielding the scroll to a huge dark-bearded man who hungrily scooped it up and swept away with it in his arms.

—*The Gift of Asher Lev*, paperback, p. 351

Should not our encounter with Scripture be a dance with the Holy Word?

There was an old folk custom, now lost in the mists of history, in which a child was formally introduced to the sweetness of the Word of God. A page of the Bible was given to the child. Upon the page was spread some honey and the child was asked to taste it. Hence from earliest youth, the child would be introduced to a positive experience of Scripture, the sweetness of the Word of God.

What else need be said?

"How sweet are thy words to my taste,
sweeter than honey to my mouth."

—Ps. 119:103, RSV

Introduction

Novelist Taylor Caldwell called Luke her "dear and glorious physician." To her, Luke is like the old fashioned family doctor, friendly, close, humane, trustworthy, and healing. St. Paul agrees when he writes, "Luke, the beloved physician, sends greetings" (Col. 4:14). Luke seems to have that much-prized quality of personal warmth and intimacy so much hungered for by the lonely people of our fast track society. He comes across as an accessible human being, someone we can confide in, a person ready to listen to us, a man who is not afraid of our problems.

Cardinal Newman has noted that Luke differs from his fellow evangelists in having received what is called a liberal education. He resembled his close friend, St. Paul, who also was privileged to have acquired a good bit of learning before embarking on his mission career. Tradition says that Luke came from Antioch, a city celebrated for the refinement of its leading citizens. As a doctor, he would have received a distinction that put him in the front ranks of his community.

It is through the prism of these attractive qualities that his gospel comes to us. Browsing through the pages of his writings, we soon feel the warmth of the man and the human appeal of the Jesus he tells us about. Luke's gospel gives us the human face of Jesus. By doing this he eases us into the mystery of Christ's divinity. In making us feel at home with the human Jesus, Luke shows us how to be intimate with the divine Christ.

Luke selects those moments in Christ's life that touch our common humanity. If Matthew gives us an infant Jesus who associates with the majestic Magi from Persia, Luke balances this scene by showing us the Jesus who met with the humble shepherds. If John's gospel soars like an eagle to discern the origin of Jesus in the heavenly realms of the Word, Luke travels a country road to a simple village, Bethlehem (House of Bread), to recover the human origins of Jesus.

Other gospels begin with theological language. Luke begins with a series of songs. Mark wants to get on with the story. Luke likes to linger on scenes, slowing the pace for meditative repose. In fact, he has so many scenes about prayer that his gospel is called the gospel of prayer.

The other evangelists seem to use events as vehicles for religious teachings. Luke is a people person, giving us a cast of characters, especially of the women who figured so prominently in Christ's ministry. He is less moralistic, yet somehow full of moral drive. It is probably no accident that Matthew's Sermon on the Mount becomes the Sermon in the Valley in Luke. He likes to downside and underplay his narrative.

The result of all this is a vividly human Jesus without any prejudice to his divinity. In a way, Luke projects a bit of himself by giving us a Jesus who is very much like the trusted family doctor, beloved and intimate.

Father Eugene La Verdiere has noted the prominence of meals in Luke's gospel. Where else is one going to feel more human, more in touch with family and community than in the intimacy of a meal? Luke presents us with a Jesus who seems to thrive on going to dinners, unguarded situations where people can be more receptive to his saving message. It is Luke who has the most beloved dinner scene in the Bible, the Emmaus meal.

The human face of Jesus at these multiple repasts glows with affection for friends, frowns in anger at hypocrisies, arches with mock despair at the follies of the guests, smiles with welcome at their virtues, and sings heartily at the festivals. Luke's Last Supper scene presents a human face of Jesus eager to save Judas and forestall Peter. Luke's meal collage of the human face of Jesus offers enough portrait materials for artists for as long as there are people trying to unravel the mystery of Jesus.

The Christ of Luke's gospel should have its own special appeal to our therapeutic minded culture. We are a health conscious people, forever taking our emotional temperatures and chronicling our cholesterol count. We seem to need a counselor for every unsettling event and an instant medical cure for every physical ailment. Happily we have sufficient humorists to curb our excesses in pursuing these otherwise valuable goals.

Jesus may not be exactly a therapist in Luke's telling of his story, but he does come through as one interested in healing the whole person. In this gospel more than the others, the healing miracles of Jesus more clearly define the ultimate healing he wants to give us, the salvation of our whole personhood.

Perhaps for this reason Luke writes the "Gospel of Mercy," or the "Gospel of the Great Pardons." For all moderns who feel a sense of lostness, there are consoling memories in Luke that persuade us that Jesus is especially interested in the lost ones. Jesus walks through Luke's gospel seeking lost people: a prodigal son, a sinful woman, the scrappy little tax collector, Zaccheus, and the good thief. Jesus likes to tell stories about lost coins and lost sheep.

Jesus' merciful concern especially reaches out to poor people. Jesus quotes in full a text from Isaiah about bringing Good News to the poor. Only in Luke does Jesus tell the story about the poor man Lazarus so insensitively ignored by the rich man. Nothing is more human about a face than one that looks with love and pity on those in need. That is the face of Jesus we see in Luke.

Yet, there is nothing sentimental about the face of Jesus in Luke. The depth we see there is the kind that draws people to discipleship — strong, not quite stern. This is the Jesus who is unafraid to ask people to leave everything to follow him. The demand of discipleship appears again and again. Leave the self. Take the cross. Follow Jesus.

Luke's Christ will ask nothing of us that he does not do himself. He tells the Emmaus disciples that there was a "must" about the cross, otherwise, there would be no entry into glory. This is a teaching Jesus had mentioned five other times in his ministry. Luke would emphasize the same teaching three times in his Acts of the Apostles. He offers us a human face of Jesus that is never soft, cloudy, vague, uncertain, tentative or unsure. At the same time it is a face that is compassionate, humorous, kind, and strong.

Yet, the Jesus of Luke is never a somber religious pedant, solemn to the point of heaviness, weighted with too much self importance. Jesus comes through these gospel pages as one with lightness of spirit, the incarnation of a biblical wisdom that finds pleasure in the company of human beings. This Jesus knows how to be happy, to be positively joyful. After all, he has so much Good News to bring. Carroll Stuhlmueller points out that Greek words for joy appear in Luke more often than the other gospels — twenty-five times in Luke, twelve times in Matthew, three times in Mark.

Such manifestations of joy on the face of Jesus are traceable to the power and presence of the Spirit. The gift of joy from the Spirit penetrates the Lucan text. Mary rejoices in the conception of Jesus through the power of the Spirit. Elizabeth exults in the visit of Mary whom Elizabeth blesses because she has believed. Jesus moves in the power of the Spirit, says with Isaiah that the Spirit is upon him, rejoices in the Spirit that the Father has revealed truth to the little ones, declares that the Spirit will give us the words we need in our time of peril.

To gaze on the human face of Jesus in Luke is to see someone who is at peace and in absolute touch with God. Jesus does not show us a face that is tormented to the edge of despair by the lack of meaning in life. Even in Luke's Way of the Cross, where the women weep over his suffering, one of them is drawn to taking a warm towel to soothe his face so that its human dignity be not marred and hidden by the blood and sweat. Tradition says this woman was Veronica and that her act was rewarded by having the imprint of Christ's face left on the towel. We will always want to see the human face of Jesus. St. Luke has guaranteed we will not be disappointed.

1 Birth Songs

Music rings from the first two chapters of Luke's gospel. On earth, Zechariah, Mary, and Simeon sing praise songs. From heaven comes the song of angels, heralding the birth of Christ. What better way to express the divine harmony than through music. Songs and hymns have strengthened faith throughout all of religious history.

An inscription on the wall of a medieval church reflects this mood. "Bach gave us God's word. Mozart gave us God's laughter. Beethoven gave us God's fire. God gave us music that we can pray without words." Luke has given us lullabies to cheer our hearts as we hum the carols of the birth of Jesus Christ and his cousin John the Baptist.

Not only music, but art encompasses Luke's birth stories. He paints word pictures to carry his story. He groups his pictures in sets of two, like altarpieces that have twin portraits. His matching pictures are like Christmas cards that tell his story in unforgettable visuals. Here are his six sets of "paintings" in his first two chapters:

1. Annunciation to Zechariah . . . Annunciation to Mary
2. Zachary's Song (Benedictus) . . . Mary's Song (Magnificat)
3. Birth/Circumcision/Naming of Baptist . . . Birth/Circumcision/Naming of Jesus
4. Hymn of the Angels . . . Hymn of Simeon
5. Mary Visits Elizabeth . . . Shepherds Visit Jesus
6. Presentation of Jesus in the Temple . . . Finding of Jesus in the Temple.

Luke's melodies and word pictures evoke a feeling for God in an experience of beauty. He also strikes a note of incomparable joy to launch his gospel. His wonderfully cheerful narrative admirably suits the happy events of God's saving works. With a song for our ears and a picture for our eyes, Luke draws us immediately into the Good News of salvation. Luke chooses the route of a poet to arouse our faith and touch our hearts. Beauty has never been put to a better service.

Zechariah Meets an Angel (Lk. 1:5-25)

Our meditation begins in the temple where the priest Zechariah offered incense, its sweet aroma enveloping the animal sacrifice, making it more pleasing to God. He and his wife, Elizabeth, belonged to the prestigious priestly family of Aaron. They endured private grief and public embarrassment because they had no children in a society that prized fertility and offspring. Advanced in years, they had no prospect of producing a child. At the same time, they were a devout couple, full of faith and leading irreproachable lives.

God chose an environment of prayer and worship to fulfill their long-held desire for a baby. As Zechariah approached the altar of incense, he met an angel standing to the right of the altar. Fear filled him. Heavenly appearances typically disturb the receiver and cause fear and apprehension. At the same time — as is clear from all of Scripture — Heaven's messengers swiftly act to dispel fear. God does not intend to scare us. The God of love does not want to frighten us, but to save us.

The angel asked Zechariah to let go of his fear. Fear, however, would constrict his heart and close his mind to the revelation of love that was about to be given. The angel's reassuring presence relaxed Zechariah and opened him to the message. God had heard the prayer of this faithful couple. Elizabeth will have a son and will name him John. The angel then told Zechariah what kind of man this boy would become. John would be a fiery prophet like Elijah was. He would call people to spiritual and moral conversion to prepare them for the Lord's coming.

Zechariah was a man of faith, but he needed to grow well beyond what he was used to. From his reading of Scripture, he knew that God had given a child to Abraham and Sarah in their old age. He did not put himself in the same exalted category as that revered couple. He knew their faith accepted God's remarkable gift. Theoretically, he knew the same could happen to him and Elizabeth, but practically, he did not believe it.

Zechariah questioned the angel about how this could happen. The angel told Zechariah that his name was Gabriel who stood in God's presence. That God had willed this birth was explanation enough. Zechariah would have to remain in the darkness of faith. Gabriel rendered Zechariah speechless, placing him in a holy silence that symbolized how faith sometimes must act in the face of divine mystery.

When they saw Zechariah, the worshipers could tell that he had received a divine visitation, both because of his tempered appearance and his enforced silence. Awe settled on them. Elizabeth conceived, went into seclusion, and praised God for this extraordinary gift. We learn from Zechariah's experience that there are times when our faith faces God hidden in a thick darkness. We put our understanding to rest in silence until God's light shows us what it all means.

Hail Mary, Full of Grace (Lk. 1:26-38)

Gabriel had a second announcement to make, this time to the virgin Mary of Nazareth, engaged to a man named Joseph. Gabriel addressed her as a highly favored one (full of grace) and a person with whom the Lord is at home. The vision troubled her but did not scare her as heavenly appearances did in other cases. The angel did not startle her. It was Gabriel's words about her special status before God that caused her concern.

It was not that Mary lacked self confidence or a had a low opinion of her dignity and self worth. Mary possessed a strong sense of self. The angel did not make her tremulous or fearful. It was Mary's down to earth humility that unsettled her. Her honest assessment of herself saw how great a love of God, self, and others she wished to attain. God's special affirmation of her dignity surprised her. It was so sudden. What did it mean?

Gabriel perceived Mary's puzzlement and — as all heavenly messengers do — strove to put her at ease. The angel told her that she will conceive a son whom she will name Jesus. He will be called the Son of the Most High, mount the throne of David, and rule over the house of Jacob. His kingdom will last forever.

This was a great deal for Mary to absorb so quickly. From her prayerful reflection on Scripture, she would have known about the messianic promises. Moreover, there was plenty of messiah talk in the air, both at the local synagogue and among her restive neighbors.

She could see that is what the angel meant. She appreciated the fact that Gabriel presented her with two astonishing revelations at once. She was about to conceive a son immediately. And that boy would grow up to be the messiah.

Like Zechariah, Mary asked how this could happen. She was pledged to marry Joseph at some future date. She had no sexual relations with him. Her question — unlike Zechariah's — arose from a fullness of faith ever in progress, not an arrested faith that needed a challenge for growth. Gabriel told her this conception would be caused by the Holy Spirit. He mentioned Elizabeth was also blessed with a pregnancy. Mary's child would be called the Son of God.

Love cannot be commanded. Love on demand is force, not affection. God has invited Mary to accept this great gift. Even God must now wait for an answer. In that silence Mary gathered up her whole soul for a response. Meditating on that moment, St. Bernard pictured the world and history waiting for a reply. Adam and Eve beg her for a yes. So also do Abraham, Moses, and David. The impatient Bernard wants her to answer quickly. "Answer with a word. Receive the Word. Speak your human word. Conceive the divine Word. Breathe a passing word. Embrace the eternal Word."

Mary understood perfectly that her answer had to arise from the deepest part of her faith life. It must be as harmonious as faith and love. As the answer coursed to her lips, it came from her heart. "Let it be done according to your word." The "let it be done" is a creation-like expression. Abraham was a father in faith who sired the first people of God. Mary is our mother in faith who will give birth to the savior and founder of a new people of God. Never has faith been more creative. Never has a faith surrender meant so much.

The Dance of John the Baptist (Lk. 1:39-56)

Thomas Merton's poem, "The Quickening of John the Baptist," retells the story of Mary's visit to her cousin Elizabeth. He pictures the newly pregnant Mary hurrying to help Elizabeth with the birth of her child. Merton sees Mary leaving behind the lemon trees, the yellow fishing boats, the oilpresses, and wine-smelling yards. Her clothes fly like sails. He asks her what truth lies behind her eyes as gray as doves.

The moment she greeted Elizabeth, the child leaped in her cousin's womb. Merton likens Mary's salutation to a monastery bell, a call to a faith experience. The unborn John wakes in his mother's body and bounds with discovery. It is a dance of faith. What was there about Mary's voice, what secret syllable awoke faith in John? What was it like to be washed in the Spirit of God while yet in the womb? How did he come to know the Jesus cloistered in the womb of Mary?

Merton required no words from John. He asked for no verbal explanations of a divine mystery. John's body talk said it all. The ecstasy of that leap in the womb — a religious dance — was its own sort of Gospel. It revealed the sheer joy of being filled with God's Spirit. Before such a mystery, we live as listeners to skies we do not at first understand with our heads, but only with our hearts. There will be time enough for teachings that spell this out. Mary, the *Theotokos* ("God Bearer"), will bring her virgin presence to us as well. Her child will wake us up and we will express our praise as joy takes hold of us.

Elizabeth then praises Mary, "Blessed are you for having believed." Mary's faith made possible God's entry of salvation and love into our human condition. She is the best faith witness we have. No other attitude will make sense of these mysterious events in Luke's infancy narrative. And no other attitude will make us happier.

Mary broke out into song and praised God with her Magnificat. She proclaimed the greatness of the Lord and attributed her joy to God. Her humility made it possible for God to fill her to the brim. People will remember her best for her faith. They will bless her because she believed. She attributes nothing to herself, but all to the achievement of the Mighty One, whose name is Holy. God has filled every age of history with mercy and never more so than now.

God ministers to the lowly and the weak and raises them up, while dispersing the arrogant and removing the powerful from their thrones. God will fill those who hunger for love, justice, and mercy with everything they dreamed of. Those who are loveless because they trust only in riches remain empty because that is what they have chosen. They were not willing to accept real riches.

Mary's song, the Magnificat, is heard every day in the church's Liturgy of the Hours at Evening Prayer. In thousands of parish rectories, convents, and monasteries — and from a multitude of homes of laity in a conscious quest for holiness — Mary's song is heard again. Its chief feature is joy.

St. Augustine says that if we were asked to sing to please a musician we would take singing lessons so as not to offend the expert. How then should we sing for God who is the world's most discriminating artist? What words would we pick? Augustine uses the example of people harvesting wheat and grapes. They sing words while they reap. Augustine often heard them in the neighboring farms and vineyards. After a while the words are not enough. The harvesters discard the restricting syllables and burst into a jubilant shout. Their cry of joy is beyond words which cannot completely express the joy in their hearts.

It is like the unrestrained roar of happiness at a victory score in a game, at the news of the end of a war, at the birth of a child, at the completion of the vows taken at a wedding or an ordination. Mary did indeed use words in her Magnificat, but the tone was radiant joy. That is what God was listening for. That is what the divine music critic wanted to hear. That is what the supreme artist did in fact hear. The point is that when we sing to God, we will please his exacting ear by our jubilant cry of joy at reaping such a harvest of love from his affectionate heart.

The Birth of John the Baptist (Lk. 1:57-80)

Elizabeth gave birth to a son. Her neighbors rejoiced with her and came to the circumcision and naming ceremony on the eighth day after the birth. They assumed that he would be called after his father, Zechariah, as was the custom. Elizabeth astonished them when she said that the boy would be called John. Since the father had control of the naming process, they looked at the mute Zechariah for confirmation. He asked for a writing tablet and wrote that the boy's name would be John.

Alex Haley, the author of the stirring book, *Roots*, a chronicle of his slave ancestry, brings us back to Africa and his tribal origins. He tells the naming story of his African progenitor, Kunta Kinte, a narrative that illumines the scene that is before us. His African ancestors also had a naming event eight days after the birth of a child. The father is expected to pick the name after much thought and prayer.

The unique feature of this approach was that the father kept the name a secret until he had whispered it into the ear of his son or daughter. The family believed the child should be the first one to hear his or her name. After breathing the new name into the ear of the child, the father raised the baby to the sky and — saying the name — intoned, "Behold, the only one greater than you."

Haley's story contains several details that echo the biblical narrative of the name of John the Baptist. The naming ceremony takes place eight days after a birth. The father chooses the name. Thirdly, the child is dedicated to God. Birth is more than a physical event; it is a spiritual moment. Luke affirms this by noting that as soon as Zechariah's tongue is loosened, the first thing he does is bless God. His holy silence is replaced by songs of joy.

Zechariah sings his own canticle of gratitude, the Benedictus. His lyrics disclose that his son will be a prophet who will herald the long expected messiah and savior. God has already produced a horn of salvation from the house of David, the child that will be born of Mary. God has kept the promise made to Abraham centuries ago that he would ultimately rescue the world from the control of evil. Since this is God's love at work in the world, the fear that troubles people will be washed away in the confident news that love will cast out fear. The tender mercy of God will visit every person like the beauty of a sunrise. Jesus will be like the dawn for every person sitting in the darkness of sadness and depression.

The mysterious event at the home of Elizabeth and Zechariah aroused awe and wonder in their neighbors. They discussed it in their kitchens, at the well, and at gatherings in the village square. The meaning of the mystery took faith to penetrate and time to absorb. It also required the unfolding of the lives of John and Jesus for its full revelation. Yet, even in those initial moments, the seed of faith began to grow as they said, "Surely, the hand of the Lord is with this child" (1:66).

Zechariah's Song, the Benedictus, is chanted each morning in the church's Liturgy of the Hours. Devoted laity, priests, male and female religious greet the dawn of each day with this praise song about God's tender mercy. Like the Magnificat, it is a jubilant shout of joy arising from hearts of faith.

Many modern people face this first chapter of Luke with bewilderment. Poetry? Yes. More likely, they tend to think, fantasy and myth. What is one to make of it? Urban, technological-minded people see the world in terms of questions to be answered and problems to be solved. Their tool for doing this is always reason and logic. Given enough time, their mental probing will answer the question and solve the problem.

The Lucan narrative says that life is much more a mystery than modern people are accustomed to affirm. In the words of novelist Flannery O'Connor, "Life is more a mystery to be reverenced than a problem to be solved." Luke unabashedly and joyously flaunts the mystery of life and calls for the faith in God that alone can penetrate it. A few faith-filled parents in a remote, ancient village grasp the importance of the most consequential births in history. Mystery does not mystify them. It energizes them. It brings them joy so strong we still sing their words. Modern people do not have to surrender the key of logic to enjoy this. They need only accept the additional key of faith to exult in the sunrise of Christ.

Reflection

1. Luke paints a series of word pictures — dual annunciations, dual births, dual temple scenes. What is the usefulness of these parallels?
2. Even though Zechariah was a true man of faith, he could not grasp the truth of the annunciation about a son. How would my faith react in his situation?
3. Much as I believe in heavenly persons, what would I feel if one appeared to me?
4. Why do most biblical people react with fear to heavenly appearances? Why do heavenly messengers work quickly to dispel such fear?
5. What is the difference in tone between Zechariah's questioning of Gabriel and that of Mary?
6. What does Mary mean when she says, "I do not know man"?

7. Augustine says that God is pleased above all by a jubilant shout of joy beyond the words of praise songs. What does he mean?
8. In what way might I participate in the church's daily Liturgy of the Hours?
9. Why do many modern people feel frustration when reading the first chapter of Luke? How might they express their feelings?
10. How have I experienced life "more as a mystery to be reverenced than a problem to be solved"?

Prayer

Lord God, revealer of mysteries, you opened the hearts of those lovely couples — Zechariah and Elizabeth, Joseph and Mary — to the wonder of births that beckoned the immediate coming of salvation to this world. Your Spirit moved them to respond with faith. Send your Spirit to us to quicken our faith as well.

2   A God in a Cave, a Child in a Temple

Jesus Is Born in David's Royal City (Lk. 2:1-7)

Luke introduces the Christmas story on a majestic note of world significance. He asks us to view the birth of Jesus from the throne of the emperor Caesar Augustus, great nephew of Julius Caesar. The emperor has ordered a census for tax purposes. Mary and Joseph must go to Bethlehem, David's royal city to be enrolled in the census.

Luke links a world ruler with Jesus' birth. The spiritual ruler born at Bethlehem will affect the secular ruler of the known world. Luke names world leaders again in telling the story of Christ's baptism in the Jordan. Christ's immersion in the Jordan will send ripples out to change the course of the Tiber. In other words, the birth and baptism of Jesus Christ will have world significance.

A second reason for invoking the name of Augustus in Christ's birth story is that he was the "Peace Emperor." He ended the civil wars that raged after the assassination of Julius Caesar and imposed a *Pax Romana* (the Roman Peace) on the world. He closed the doors of the Janus shrine, whose portals were open in wartime. He erected a Peace Altar and promoted the cause of a world without war. Greek cities celebrated his birthday as their new year and called him the "savior of the world."

Augustus imposed peace by force. Jesus initiated peace through freedom based on love and forgiveness. The greater peace was the *Pax Christi* because it affected the inner self as well as the outer society. The origin of the most profound peace was occurring in Bethlehem, not in Rome.

In the Acts of the Apostles, we see the Christian mission going from Judea to Syria to Rome. In this birth story we witness a reversal of geography, as the movement is from Rome to Syria (where

Quirinius is governor) to Judea's Bethlehem. Acts ends with the preaching of the risen savior in Rome. Luke's gospel begins with the birth of the savior in Bethlehem, a birth that will one day affect Rome. The least of the cities of Judea, the most inconsequential village in the world will touch and change the greatest one — Rome.

Now Joseph and Mary came to Bethlehem and looked for a place to stay. The public inn was one large room where the lodgers slept on cots raised above the floor by a small platform. Their animals slept on the floor itself. Because of the large crowd already arrived for the census, no room was available at the inn. The local synagogue provided shelter in a room under its main building. That too was filled.

Joseph and Mary may have contacted their distant relatives there, but apparently with little success. The people of Bethlehem showed a heartless lack of hospitality to a pregnant woman. The Royal city of David refused a welcome to the newest, greatest, and eternal heir to David's throne. The throne of David was not open to David's legitimate successor. Whenever we fail to show hospitality to anyone, we repeat the coarse sin of the callous people of Bethlehem that night. Whenever we refuse to welcome Jesus into our own hearts, we play out again the sad story of those who physically turned away a worried Joseph and a pregnant Mary that holy night.

Joseph and Mary had to find some shelter quickly for Mary was about to give birth. Christian tradition has identified a cave as the site of Jesus' birth. A basilica was built over it in 325. Today, in a chamber beneath the church, a pilgrim sees a marble chapel with a hole in the floor. A gold plated star surrounds the opening. Around the star are found the words, "Hic natus est, Jesus Christus, Salvator Mundi" — Here was born Jesus Christ, the savior of the world. Pilgrims may put their hands into the opening and touch the earth beneath, the earth upon which it is believed that Jesus Christ was born.

Then Mary gave birth to Jesus and wrapped him in swaddling clothes and laid him in a manger — a food bin. Francis of Assisi pictured the manger as a cradle and that is how we have thought about it ever since. That his first cradle was a food container is not without its symbolism. Jesus would one day call himself the Bread of Life. Manger food nourished the ox and the ass. Christ-bread will nourish human souls. The symbolism contains an added richness when we recall that Bethlehem means "House of Bread." Here at the beginning of Luke's gospel, shepherds will recognize Jesus the Bread of Life in Bethlehem. At the end of Luke's gospel, two disciples recognize Jesus in the Breaking of the Bread at Emmaus.

Which brings us to the shepherds. It has been suggested that the shepherds who were watching their flocks that night belonged to a special order. Every morning and evening an unblemished lamb was offered at the temple. Temple officials retained their own flocks in order to have a steady supply of "perfect lambs." It is possible that these shepherds were in the employ of the temple administration. If this be so, then the shepherds who looked after the temple lambs were the first to see the Lamb of God who takes away the sins of the world.

The Carol of the Angels (Lk. 2:8-14)

In any case, the shepherds were blessed with the appearance of an angel and surrounded by the glory of the Lord. Like an imperial messenger proclaiming the birth of a new emperor, the angel announced to the shepherds the birth of the savior. As in all such revelations, there was fear in the recipients and an effort on the part of the revealer to dispel the fear.

In Luke's narrative, the Christmas angel is the first evangelist. This angel speaks of a Gospel, of Good News of salvation that will be brought by Jesus who is messiah and Lord. The angel's announcement was like that of Isaiah's prophecies of the birth of a messiah in 9:5ff and 40:9-11.

Local custom called for musicians to come to a home where a new birth occurred and greet the newborn baby with welcome songs. At the shepherds' fields, a multitude of angels filled the sky and supplied the music that normally would be sung by the neighbors. Angels celebrated the birth of Jesus with the words, "Glory to God in the highest and on earth peace (2:14). On Palm Sunday the disciples will sing to Jesus on the eve of his death: "Peace in heaven and glory in the highest" (19:38). The angels and the disciples open and close the historical ministry of Jesus like antiphonal singers in choir stalls.

The Adoration of the Shepherds (Lk. 2:15-20)

A shepherd's life was lonely, poor, and dangerous. A shepherd lived outdoors, facing the twists and turns of the seasons and the threats from wild animals. Often a shepherd learned how to turn his loneliness into a meditative solitude. A shepherd had the best chance for understanding and praying the Psalms of David, himself a shepherd.

No one was closer to reality than a shepherd, yet he was also attuned to the mystery of nature and of God. The more a shepherd butted his head against reality, the more he realized how mysterious it all was. He had his sheep, his stars, and his pastures. He loved his flock and his God. It was to men like these that the angels came on Christmas night. It was such men who were the first to meet the savior of the world.

After the angels disappeared, the shepherds searched for and found the cave where Jesus was born. In their act of adoration, the shepherds simply and directly gazed into the mystery of the Christ Child. Angels guided their perceptions. They saw a God who could hold the world in his hands, now unable even to enfold the heads of the cattle with his tiny human hands. They beheld the God upon whom they depended for life, turn to his mother's breast for the milk of survival. They stared at the author of the sun's heat and noticed he felt a chill until the swaddling robes were tucked around him again. The all-powerful one looked helpless. The very source of light accepted the shadows imposed by the night. Reality's greatest free spirit put up with the annoyances of human limits.

The shepherds contemplated this mystery and rested in it. Their life experiences had taught them to be at ease with spiritual reality. They did not torture seeming contradictions to death. They allowed them to open up new sources of light and love. That is why their appearance at the birth scene was so relaxing and appropriate. The first ones invited to the birthing celebration were persons whose faith and love would best appreciate what was going on.

The shepherds' capacity to absorb these amazing contrasts sustain the secret of the Christmas story. That is their Christmas gift to us. If we forget the God in the cave, we reduce the Bethlehem event to a charming birth scene with no special meaning. If we saw only God, we would endow the setting with an aura of magic and myth and rob it of any historical or salvational significance. Christmas just is not Christmas if these paradoxes — seeming contradictions — are denied or ignored.

The Christmas story invites us to come with faith to behold the God-man in the cave. It is not enough to simply admire the child, for who cannot but be moved by the intrinsic wonder of a new baby. But the shepherds did more than that. They worshiped the child with their faith. We could sing nursery rhymes at the manger cradle. We should imitate the shepherds who crooned the song of the angels about glory in the highest and peace on earth. The maternal in us wants to simply rock the cradle. With the shepherds we must also believe this cradle will rock the world.

The proud, who know everything, will miss the point of Christmas. The shepherds who are humble enough to know that they do not know everything, will find the living truth in Jesus. The strong who trust only in power, will dismiss the very idea of the vulnerability of a God-child. The shepherds, who represent the poor, the suffering, the despised, the desperate and disturbed, accept the wonder of One who accepts such a lowly condition and identifies with their sorrows. Such a One can heal them.

The ancient Romans built a pantheon for all the gods of the world. They invited the Christians to put a statue of Jesus in there with the other gods. "Be open minded. Join the fellowship of world religions." The Christians said "No thanks," because that meant Jesus would be robbed of the uniqueness of his divinity and his saving work. He alone is the world's real savior.

History repeats itself today as unbelievers strive to build a pantheon for the world's greatest men and women. They invite today's Christians to enshrine Jesus as the Great Moral Teacher, as though that was the essence of his mission. Again, Christians must reply firmly with a loving "No" because Jesus is more than that. Jesus is God-man and savior.

With the shepherds we kneel in the cave at Bethlehem and worship the God-man in the cave. We echo the song of the angels by praising God's glory and begging for peace on earth and in our own hearts. We gaze at the humility of Jesus and pray that our own pride will melt away. We behold the vulnerability of the child and hope that our own foolish defensiveness will sink into the sea. As we admire Jesus' willingness to be dependent on his parents, we affirm again our wish to be dependent on God. As we contemplate a God who is willing to accept the limits of the earthly condition, we open ourselves to an honest embrace of life's boundaries. We will discover that the moment we do all these things, a surge of unsuspected freedom fills us, a strength greater than any derived from our valued independence engulfs us, and an inner sense of peace — so long hoped for — enters our hearts at last. We pray with the shepherds, "O hold Jesus tenderly, dear mother, for he rules our hearts."

The Christ Child is born again today in the lonely, the sick, the poor, the dying, and the forgotten. He asks us to love him by loving and serving them. That is how we fill every day with the warmth of Christmas.

The Presentation in the Temple (Lk. 2:21-40)

Eight days after his birth Jesus was circumcised and formally given the name of Jesus as Gabriel had instructed Mary in the Annunciation. Some time later Joseph and Mary brought Jesus to the temple to dedicate him to the Lord. They made an offering of a pair of turtledoves, the modest sacrifice of the poor. Just as they had obeyed the Roman law by traveling to Bethlehem for the census, so now they fulfill the Mosaic law by journeying to the temple for Mary's purification and Christ's presentation.

At the completion of their rituals, they were met by an old man named Simeon. Luke describes him as a holy man, devoted to prayer and waiting for the arrival of the consolation of Israel. He was part of a devout group known as the "Quiet Ones." In solitude they sought in prayer the hope of salvation. They had no interest in political or military solutions to the sorrows of their people. They chose prayer as the best route to the future hope.

The Holy Spirit filled this man and revealed to him that he would see the messiah before he died. The Spirit brought him to the temple that day and led him to the couple who held Jesus in their arms. He took the child into his own arms and began to sing.

Simeon's song, the "Nunc Dimittis" (Now dismiss your servant), is the death song of this old gentleman. He has completed his life's goal by seeing the messiah. He found the child in the arms of poor people making the offering of the poor. In the sunset of his own life, he encountered the sunrise of the world. In the evening of his life, he was fortunate enough to behold a new day. As he cradled Jesus in his arms, he swayed with joy. From Simeon Jesus heard the first human hymn that was composed out of love for him. Simeon could now die in peace, because he had seen the savior of the world.

Simeon then turned to Mary and told her that her son would be a sign of contradiction in his lifetime. Moreover, she would experience deep sorrow along with her son. A messiah cannot expect to have an easy future. His mother will grieve as she sees the pain her son will endure. Simeon's somber prediction introduced a shadow into what was otherwise a scene of light and happiness.

He left the young couple to brood over the fate of their baby, joyful in having him, chilled about what lay ahead. Then an old prophetess, a widow named Anna, came to cheer them up. With a great smile on her face and arms outspread she embraced them and praised God for their child. They returned to Nazareth and watched their child grow strong, filled with wisdom and God's favor.

The Finding in the Temple (Lk. 2:41-52)

Each year, Joseph and Mary made a pilgrimage to Jerusalem for the Passover. When Jesus was twelve-years-old, the age at which he officially reached manhood, he went up with his parents as was their custom. At the end of the feast, the women's caravan left first because they traveled more slowly. The men's group left a little later and caught up the with the women at the evening encampment. Jesus had lingered at the temple, having become part of the lively exchange on religious topics between other young men and the rabbis.

Joseph and Mary, each thinking their son was with the other parent, did not miss him until they met that evening. They searched in vain for him among their relatives and acquaintances. They returned to Jerusalem to find him deeply engaged with the religion teachers, listening to them and asking them questions. Everyone there was astounded that such a young man could grasp the issues with such understanding and could give such profound answers to questions addressed to him.

His parents were equally astonished, but they commented only on the deep worry he had caused them. "Your father and I have been looking for you with great anxiety" (verse 48). Like any distraught parents they asked him why he had done this to them. Now we hear the first quoted words of Jesus Christ. "Why were you looking for me? Did you not know that I must be in my Father's house" (verse 49). Neither Joseph nor Mary understood his reply. They would not be the first parents in history to shake their heads in bewilderment at their offspring's behavior and explanations, even one so august as Jesus.

Jesus healed the pain and misunderstanding, not by further explanations, but by obediently returning with them to Jerusalem. This is the last we hear from him until eighteen years later when he began his public ministry. Mary did not forget the experience. She meditated on it over the years in her heart. During the thirty years of the "hidden life," those quiet years at Nazareth, Mary was in daily contact with the human incarnation of the Son of God.

Humanly she treated him as any loving mother would. In faith, she took in the mystery of her son as it came to her in the thousands of daily exchanges. Scripture draws the veil over those years of communion in which mother shaped son and the son's mystery revealed itself to her. Like any mother she was pleased to see him grow in wisdom and age. Like the greatest believer who ever lived, she enjoyed seeing Jesus advance in favor before God and people.

Reflection

1. In what ways can I experience a rebirth of Jesus' influence in my life?
2. What are ways we can fail today to have no room in the inn for Jesus?
3. The manger was used as a food container. What symbolism does this suggest as it became Christ's cradle?

4. A shepherd had to be a realist because of his profession. Yet he came to see the mystery of life in being so realistic. How could that happen? Has it been my experience?
5. Our meditation on the adoration of the shepherds notes that they encountered the paradoxes — seeming contradictions — in the Bethlehem cave. What are some other "paradoxes" our faith encounters? What are we supposed to do with seeming contradictions?
6. Luke fills his infancy narrative with many songs. What are my favorite Christmas carols and what do they tell me about Jesus and my living out my Christianity?
7. What does the Simeon story have to say to me?
8. The story of the Finding in the Temple says that Jesus grew in age, grace, and wisdom before God and people. How do I grow in age, grace, and wisdom?
9. Mary learned a lot from Jesus in the thirty years of the hidden life. Jesus learned a lot from her. What does this tell me?
10. What part of the Christmas story do I like best? Why?

Prayer

New born Jesus, I will look for you among all the poor, the lonely and the helpless. I will love you and serve you in them. I will sing to you and show you affection in them and all whom I meet. With your grace I know this will be possible.

3 John's No-Nonsense Message

John Is the Voice — Christ Is the Word (Lk. 3:1-6)

St. Luke loved history. He enjoyed identifying a turning point in history. To him, the career of John the Baptist was a benchmark in history. Luke ranked John the Baptist with the major historical figures of his time. Luke was not one bit shy about placing John in the company of the most powerful people in his world.

Luke lists the Baptist in the company of the six principal political and religious leaders of his age.

(1) Tiberius Caesar — the second emperor of Rome
(2) Pontius Pilate — the Roman governor of Galilee
(3) Herod — the Jewish governor of Galilee
(4) Philip — Herod's brother and governor of Trachonitis
(5) Lysanius — Tetrarch of Abilene
(6) Caiphas — High Priest of the Jewish community (Annas was his father-in-law, the power that supported him)

Luke takes an unknown young man from an obscure backwater of a Roman province and places him in this impressive assembly of VIP's. We see the Baptist ranking with the power elite. Why does Luke do this? Because the message of John would have an impact on world history. As a prophet he would alert his listeners to the arrival of the world's savior. This savior would shake the throne of Tiberias, rattle Pilate's nerves in the Fortress Antonia, confront the three Jewish governors and upset the dreams of the High Priest of Israel. John's message announced a change in the very course of human and religious history itself.

Once Luke has raised our awareness to the level of world history, he quotes John's appeal to prepare for this new situation. Now that the guest list of emperors, governors and top priests swims into our minds, we are reminded of the special treatment these leaders receive.

Level the hills. Fill in the valleys. Repair the roads. Pare down the bumps. Stuff the potholes with earth. Fashion a smooth road for the coming of the emperor, the governor, the priest.

If that is what one does for this world's bosses, should there not be an even greater preparation for the world's savior?

The Baptist does not put himself in such great company, but he does draw attention to this important moment in history. He tells us about a person who is more important than Caesar, Pilate, or Caiphas. John is not interested in road crews, physically easing the bumps for traveling celebrities. He speaks of opening a spiritual road to our hearts. "Mend your lives. Take down the walls of selfishness. Fill in the hollows of self pity. Be open to Christ's coming."

The imagery of preparing for the arrival of famous people is well known to us today. Air Force One and a legion of Secret Service personnel sweep everything and everyone aside for the coming of the American president. Television interrupts normal programming to bring us the media hype accompanying his arrival.

It is the same for our globetrotting popes. We see the plane, the carpet, the kissing of the earth, the crowds, the pope mobile.

The immense preparations needed to receive a pope or a president in our dangerous and complicated world offer us an image of what John the Baptist asks us to do when preparing for the coming of the King of Kings and Lord of Lords. We do not need the protective ministrations of the Secret Service. We do require the safeguards of a life morally renewed. We do not have to drill ourselves to look great in front of a camera. We must touch up the face of our souls so they look (and are) welcoming to the arrival of Jesus.

In the Liturgy of the Hours, the Office of Readings for the Third Sunday of Advent, St. Augustine gives us a marvelous meditation contrasting John the Baptist as a Voice and Jesus as the Word. John calls himself the Voice crying in the desert. But a voice, of itself, is just sound. If the voice is to make sense, it must utter words. John the Baptist lets us know that the only way his Voice makes sense is because it speaks the Word which is Christ.

John's Voice is temporary. Christ the Word is eternal. John simply makes a sound. Christ provides the meaning. John's sound reaches the ear of the listener. The Christ Word pierces the heart of the hearer. Sound vanishes. Word remains. Voice and ear are but delivery systems meant to reach the heart.

In a communication event, I want to reach you. I have a word in my heart that I wish were in yours. I need my voice to carry that word. When there is true communion, my voice carries the word, which ideally fades away and my word rests in your heart.

The word and the voice seem to be identified. Many of those listening to John thought he was the messiah. His Voice was so powerful. But John reminded them that he was only a sound. The Word was Jesus. John was merely the Voice that prepared people for the Word. He asked his listeners to empty themselves so they could be filled with Christ. By his own witness of humility, he showed how this emptying took place. We next see how this was to be done.

The Need For Personal Transformation (Lk. 3:7-18)

The centerpiece of the Baptist's preaching was conversion. His goal was the conversion of the whole person, not just the mind. He was not interested in debating disputed religious questions. His passion was the moral and spiritual transformation of a person. He was forceful, but he never compelled his hearers to believe. The messiah will come to free us from sin and all other oppressions. But we must be willing to change. Jesus will not convert anyone who does not wish it.

The Baptist approached conversion from four points of view.

1. *He invited his listeners to a freely willed conversion to the person of Jesus Christ.* Some people start with the message of Jesus and then go to the person. But it seems better to build the bonds of affection for Jesus and then establish the ties of doctrine. The personal experience of Jesus leads to a true appreciation of his message.

2. *John urged his audiences to honestly acknowledge their sins and turn away from them.* "You brood of vipers!" (verse 7). Sins destroy the growth and happiness of the person and erode the possibilities of wholesome friendships. Sin harms people and undermines true love of self, God, and others. Later on, the apostles would follow John's approach, arousing in people a sense of their sinfulness and then offering them the Good News of Christ who saves them from their sins.

3. *He tried to give people a living feeling of the powerful presence of God, acting in their lives and in the world around them.* This is the loving presence of an affectionate divine person who

wants each of us to be happy and to have peace of heart. This presence will be embodied for them in the person of Jesus. When this divine love is felt and experienced, then the receiver will have a more intense reason for letting go of evil and turning to Love.

4. *The Baptist is strong in asserting the judgement of God.* "Who warned you to flee from the coming wrath?" (verse 7). God will expect us to be accountable. The Lord will offer an abundance of love, graces, and spiritual gifts. If we fail to accept this love and if we are too timid about sharing and using our gifts, then we face the judgement of God. John used strong language to remind his people of the judgement. He told them the axe was headed for the root of the tree of their lives. If they did not show the fruits of moral behavior, they would be cut down and thrown into the fire.

They cannot claim immunity from judgement just because they were the offspring of Abraham, the chosen ones of God. Mere biological connection is not enough. Ethnic membership in a culture or even official membership in a religion is insufficient. The acquisition of moral character and spiritual depth is what counts. After all God made people from clay. Pointing to the rocks, John forcefully told them that the Lord could raise up children of Abraham from those stones.

People who speak with conviction will attract attention. John's powerful moral voice drew crowds to the banks of the Jordan. His fiery sermons spoke to something very real in their lives. He moved them to a desire to change. "What shall we do," asked the crowds. John challenged them to acts of charity and social concern. They should clothe the poor and feed the hungry.

Tax collectors asked him for instruction and guidance. They knew that people hated them for collaborating with the Roman government. They also exploited their own people, increasing their take by adding hidden costs for their services as tax agents. John did not tell them to give up their jobs, but he did command them to stop cheating people. They should not use their authority to take more money than was allowed by the law.

Soldiers asked John for moral instruction. As troops of occupation, they found numerous ways to intimidate and bleed the local people. John confronted them with their well known crimes of violently robbing farmers and villagers and of using false witnesses to extort money from small businesses. He snapped the spell of their greed by telling them, "Be satisfied with your wages."

John touched a great many of his listeners. He converted their hearts and watched with joy as they waded into the Jordan for his baptism. Songs of praise arose from Jordan's banks as the stream of penitents let the waters wash them with a ritual cleansing and give them a new sense of how to live before God.

So exciting was John that many people wondered if he were the expected messiah. John quickly disabused them of this misperception. He approved their expectation, denied that he was the messiah and told them that one "mightier than I was coming." Cupping the river water in his hands he told them he only baptized with water. The messiah would baptize with the Holy Spirit and fire.

The "I" language found in all the gospel stories about the Baptist deserves a brief meditation. Essentially, the Baptist asked people to abandon their egotism to find their real selves, their true personhood, their "I." The ego is an image of the spirit of the world. The person — the "I" — is an image of the Holy Spirit of God.

The obsessions of the ego hide the reality of the person. The ego is cultivated and made strong by conformity to the standards of the world. Yet the ego never makes us feel happy or at peace. The ego causes us to feel inadequate, ill at ease with ourselves, anxious, hostile, and depressed. And matters get worse the more the ego is nourished. A powerful ego makes us feel weak. That is why the ego drives us to get more and more power over others to compensate for the weakness felt. This is what produces maniacal dictators, tyrants, and ruthless people of all kinds.

On the other hand, the person (the real me) discovers far greater power in loving communion with the standards of God. When the person advances in loving union with God, enduring peace floods the heart, harmony with others becomes possible, anxiety diminishes and a sense of power develops. This is the power of love, not of force. It is the power of freedom not of addiction or compulsion.

A person in love with God has no need to push others around, hurt them, cheat them, lie to them, rape them, humiliate them, take revenge against them. Love of God makes the self feel strong and adequate for the challenges of life. Domination needs expand because the ego has no other way of staying alive. Control needs evaporate when God's creative love nourishes the real me.

At the core of the teachings of John the Baptist is conversion from the slavery of the ego to the freedom of the person. John asks us to detach ourselves from our ego and its sins of selfishness, cheating, violence, force, and all other forms of cruelly controlling others.

Detachment from the ego reveals the existence of the person. But there is yet another step. "I" am not a stand-alone unit. The loop is completed when I *attach* myself to Christ. The more I am other-centered in Christ, the more will my full personhood flourish and become powerful. That is what St. Paul meant when he said, "I have the strength for everything through him who empowers me" (Phil. 4:13). When the Gospel uses empowerment language it is not using a political strategy such as is common today. The Gospel speaks only of the empowerment of love that comes only from attachment to Christ.

It is not enough to discover the "I" by detachment from the ego. I must also attach myself to one "mightier than I." Thus the *process of detachment from ego to attachment to Christ* constitutes the fullness of the direction given by the Baptist. In his message about losing the self (read "ego"), Jesus would teach exactly the same message at far greater length. All the gospels illuminate in a variety of ways this powerful lesson about personal change.

The Baptism and Genealogy of Jesus (Lk. 3:21-38)

In the middle of describing John's ministry at the Jordan, Luke inserts a notice about Herod's arrest of the Baptist. John had publicly denounced Herod for seducing Herodias away from her husband (who was Herod's step-brother) and marrying her. Worse yet, she was also his niece because she was the daughter of another step-brother. The marriage outraged Jewish sensitivities and broke their religious and civil laws. John's impolitic and dangerous denunciation landed him in jail and led to his ultimate martyrdom.

Luke resumes the narrative of John's Jordan ministry with the story of the baptism of Jesus. The cousins meet. Traditional Christian imagery has imagined John as the lamp meeting Christ the sun, the Voice encountering the Word, the one who leaped in the womb standing before the one who was adored in the womb. Jesus descended into the tomb of the waters where he symbolically buried sinful humanity.

Jesus then arose from the waters and we arose with him. In a sense this was a dress rehearsal for the death and resurrection of Jesus. The book of Genesis taught that an angel with a flaming sword closed us out from the gates of Paradise. Over the centuries, biblical people imagined that Paradise was in the third heaven, sealed from human view by the sky. The first heaven was the atmosphere below the sky and above the earth. The second heaven was the sky itself, thought to be a great solid cover over the earth. Paradise — God's home — was above that. Like the angel with a fiery sword, the gates of the sky kept us away from Paradise.

Thus God was "up there," lost from human contact due to sinfulness. But that changed at Christ's baptism. When he rose from the waters he was bathed by a heavenly light that shone from beyond the sky, for it was torn open by divine love. The sky parted. The gates of Paradise opened allowing heaven's light to encompass Jesus and all those present at the baptismal scene.

Jesus was to baptize in Spirit and in fire, hence the Spirit comes accompanied by the incandescent light of God. God the Father's voice is heard affirming the sonship of Jesus and the divine pleasure in his forthcoming ministry. In Noah's time, a dove had come to the ark to signal the end of the flood and the arrival of a new harmony between God and people. Now the Spirit descends in bodily form, like a dove, and hovers over Jesus to honor him who is at one with God and to forecast the reconciliation between God and people that would result from his life, death, and resurrection.

This biblical sound and light experience illumines the call each of us received in our own baptisms. Christ washed us clean then and continues to do so, provided we are open to the lifelong conversion to which he calls us. Jesus wants us to be a loving force in our families and communities, lights shining in our daily encounters with others. Each of us will be a radiant light of love when we stand beside Christ, our source of light. With him we will be bathed in the glory that broke through the open sky at the Jordan.

For one brief and shining moment, the pure and dazzling light of the Trinity settled on the Jordan that day long ago, causing awe and wonder in those privileged to be there. In faith, especially in the sacramental celebration of Christ's baptism, one week after Epiphany, we can re-experience that mystery and revelation. We may receive a ray of that splendor to carry us through our own journey to the day when we shall experience it permanently in eternal life.

Springs of water were made holy when Christ revealed his glory to the world at the Jordan. Jesus calls us to draw the waters of love from the fountains of his spirit. On our baptismal day, he burned away our guilt by fire and the Holy Spirit. Our best response is praise and thanks to Christ and a commitment to share the light of love with all those we meet.

Reflection

1. Luke "name drops" famous people in his introduction to John the Baptist's ministry. Why did Luke do it?
2. How do I prepare for Christ's coming to my heart, especially in Advent?
3. Augustine says John is the "Voice" and Christ is the "Word." What does Augustine mean?
4. Why is it important to emphasize people's freedom when inviting them to accept Christ?
5. What conversion-to-Christ stories can I share that illustrate a moral change as part of their experience?
6. The Baptist speaks of divine judgement and moral accountability. Why do many people today ignore or deny divine judgement?
7. People who speak with conviction attract attention. What can I do to speak "convincingly" about Jesus?
8. If the real me is an image of God and my ego is an image of the spirit of the world, how can I overcome my ego so the real me can grow in God's image?
9. My ego wants to control others. What examples of this do I find in my own life?
10. What is the main challenge Jesus calls me to in his baptism?

Prayer

Eternal Word, you were humble enough to let the human voice of John the Baptist prepare people for your coming. Make me a voice that is so filled with you that people will be led to your love by its joyful sharing of the Gospel.

4   A Life Plan to Counter Temptation

The First Temptations of Christ (Lk. 4:1-13)

Some people cheerfully say the best way to cope with a temptation is to give into it.

Luke's account of the first temptations of Christ tells us that the best way to treat them is to defeat them.

Temptations to sin lure us into self destructive behavior. Our best response is self transformation. Only powerful self change withstands the destructive seduction of evil.

Luke shows us the sources of spiritual energy that empowered Jesus to turn away the tempter. They generated a positive spiritual environment whose gathering force overwhelmed the chaos of the tempter.

None of this happened suddenly or magically. Luke speaks of a forty day process because the gathering of inner spiritual power takes time. We see Jesus going to the desert for this lengthy period of inner growth. In the desert Jesus experienced silence, solitude, fasting, prayer, and the creative presence of the Holy Spirit. These five elements shaped the environment for the inner convergence of his energies. They served him more than adequately when he faced the tempter.

How would those very same five features form our inner lives so we can resist the evil temptations we face?

(1) Silence. External silence turns our attention to the inner noises we usually never notice. It invites us to begin our "noise abatement" procedures. Exterior quiet helps us let go of the "twenty-four hour movie" that keeps running inside our heads. Outward silence is a step toward inner quiet.

This is not mere quiet for its own sake. This is more than a stress reduction exercise, desirable as that obviously is. Inner calm's ultimate goal puts us in touch with the divine energy that can only be communicated in the spiritual side of our lives. A spiritual giver needs a spiritual receiver. Heart can only speak to heart.

Once we stop listening to the clamor of the noisy tapes in our heads and laugh away their insistent cries for our attention as though they were spoiled and petulant children, we can begin to listen to the healing voice of the Holy Spirit. The calming voice of the Spirit invites us to our most inward center of energy which is so helpful for resisting our temptations successfully.

(2) Solitude. We will derive enormous benefit from a regular experience of solitude. Some find this when they take a quiet walk or even a slow paced jog. Others discover it during the drive to and from work. A fair number make religious retreats. Despite the busyness of life, inventive people will claim a zone of solitude.

Many people today lament their loneliness. "I'm lonely. I'm surrounded by people, but I feel isolated, like a traffic cop. I have no human contact with this river of humanity." It may seem like a contradiction, but people who learn to enjoy real solitude have a better chance of establishing warm, vital human relationships.

Solitude differs from loneliness. Lonely people ache for company, for a hug, for the simple pleasure of idly passing time with a real friend. Productive solitude is a genuine path to satisfying this legitimate human hunger. There is a way of being alone that is self renewing. Scientists, artists and writers all tell stories of a burst of creativity that was nursed by solitude.

The ability to be alone reveals the secret of how to have satisfying human contact. We come out of our solitude with arms wide open to hug someone else, with a tongue ready to cheer up and comfort another, with the inner peace that helps others join us for a pleasant, restful passing of time. Solitude takes our minds off our own aches and makes them attentive to the needs of others.

(3) Fasting. Interior change rarely happens without fasting. Gandhi used the fast to intensify his "soul force." Everyone knows that dieting slims the body and focuses the mind. Fasting for a religious purpose vastly increases the attentive power of the self. But fasting is more than a concentration booster. The real issue here is

the reason for attentiveness, which is the capacity to hear the inner call of the Holy Spirit.

Religious fasting is to the soul what aerobic exercise is to the body. Fitness experts speak of the "training effect" one receives from regular exercise. The elevation of the pulse rate for twenty minutes or more creates, over a period of time, a stronger body that is able to perform daily tasks with less effort. Religious fasting produces a similar "training effect" in the soul when the person is thereby led to draw divine energy from the Spirit, an energy that never seems more powerful than when it is used to resist temptations to self destructive immoral behavior.

(4) Prayer. The fourth part of the program for inner renewal is prayer and meditation. Silence, solitude, and fasting create a productive withdrawal that is an excellent preparation for prayerful attentiveness to God. People who pray and meditate on a regular basis strike us as being "deep." The impression is not misleading, for such people do in fact sink into regions of their inner space that others barely realize exist.

Probing outer space has now become a commonplace. Taking a journey within to our inner space is less usual, but just as possible and available for everyone. One does not have to belong to an elite corps of spiritual astronauts to drop into the endless regions of our own souls which contain just as many wonders as the stars in the sky. And just as it demands night to see the stars, so also it requires darkness to see the lights of Christ within the infinite avenues of our inner selves.

And just as there is nothing frightening about the night that delights us with cosmic lights, so there is nothing to dread about entering the inner darkness, because very soon we see the light of Christ we never suspected was there. Jesus has sent us the Holy Spirit as our reassuring guide in this journey and we walk within with a pleasing sense of joy and discovery we never dreamed was possible.

This gift is available to all people and is not restricted to specialists, geniuses, saints, mystics, theologians, monks, nuns, priests, popes, or bishops. Every baptized Christian has this gift immediately, joyously and exuberantly. Those who take this spiritual adventure look on temptation in a different light, not fearfully or timidly, but with energy and power. This is a hero journey where the dragons of evil can be slain and the Holy Grail can be obtained.

The account of the first temptations of Jesus contain these five gifts which enabled him to conquer Satan. The cumulative impact of silence, solitude, fasting, prayer, and responsiveness to the Spirit occasioned Christ's triumph over the tempter. The story proves that Jesus was human enough to be tempted. It also demonstrates that Jesus modeled for us a hero journey that is just as available to us as it was to him. He felt the emotional pull to evil. He encountered the tendency of his intellect to want to justify giving into the temptations. But by adhering faithfully to the five step plan for gathering up all his inner resources, he witnessed for us what we ourselves can do just as well and effectively with the help of his Holy Spirit. Christ's love is with us to overcome evil.

Jesus gave us a spiritual plan for a spiritual battle. He worked in cooperation with the Spirit. So should we. Our ultimate victory over evil means we are liberated from self-destructive behavior and from malicious harming of other people. On a more positive note, this means we are freed to love self, others, and God and to perform each small act of our daily lives with great love.

Jesus Preaches in His Home Town Synagogue (Lk. 4:14-30)

Fortified by his profound experience in the desert, Jesus began his ministry with enthusiasm. Along the shores of Galilee and in the hill town villages, he went to the synagogues where he shared the Good News of salvation. His listeners loved him and his message. But when he came to his home town of Nazareth he met a different response in their synagogue.

A synagogue was a simple, unadorned meeting room for prayer and religious instruction. People sat around a small platform on which was a chair and a reading stand. The service was composed of four parts, (1) Opening Prayer (2) Reading from the Bible (3) A sermon (4) A Discussion. The synagogue administrator oversaw the proceedings. The day that Jesus came to the Nazareth synagogue was a day filled with unusual expectation.

Everyone knew him and his family. He had been a respected carpenter among them for many years. His widowed mother was an honored member of the community. The people heard glowing reports of what an extraordinary speaker he turned out to be. Admiring comments about him flowed in from all over Galilee. They anticipated a satisfying prayer meeting with one of their own who had made such an impressive mark elsewhere.

After the prayer, the administrator gave Jesus a scroll on which was written chapter 61 of Isaiah. Jesus read the Hebrew words and then recited them in Aramaic, for most of the listeners no longer understood the ancient Hebrew, speaking rather the dialect now known as Aramaic.

He closed the scroll, gave it back to the presiding officer and sat down to deliver his sermon. The verse he had read spoke of the Spirit anointing the messiah for the purpose of preaching Good News to the poor. It was a preaching matched by good works, such as liberating the imprisoned, healing the blind, freeing the oppressed, witnessing that in fact the messiah had indeed arrived. These words gripped the hearts of the listeners because they ached for the fulfillment of that prophecy in a time when their whole experience was one of oppression, both from the Romans and from the Jewish rulers who collaborated with the oppressors.

Many of them had relatives and friends who languished in prisons for defying the army of occupation. They felt the sting and humiliation of not being masters in their own homes. The impulse to revolution and uprising was close to their hearts. The preaching of John the Baptist revived the longing for the messiah and persuaded them that the hour was at hand.

Jesus knew very well the explosive political context that gave urgency to the words of Isaiah. But he was not interested in political rebellion. He came to preach the real meaning of Isaiah, which was the Kingdom of God, the rule of love, justice, and mercy in each human heart. He paused after the reading and allowed the intense eyes of the participants to fix themselves on him. He let the silence gather up the force of Isaiah's words and intensify the expectation of his listeners.

Then he spoke the electrifying words, "Today this scripture passage is fulfilled in your hearing" (verse 21). The messiah was here. Liberation was at hand.

Luke notes that the listeners were amazed at the words of grace that flowed from Jesus. Then it dawned on them that Jesus was applying the text to himself and his ministry. Much as they wanted a messiah they could not believe it would be Jesus. They knew him too well. Was he not the son of Joseph and Mary?

Worse yet, he was defining messiahship in spiritual terms. God's real rule was liberation from oppression here by the spiritual means of love, justice, and mercy, not by the sword and popular uprising. The Kingdom of God was a divine reality that would free them from all that oppressed them, especially personal sin. Its fulfillment would occur both here and hereafter.

Jesus saw that they understood him very well and could not accept his message. They judged he had the right theme with the wrong application. He told them that a prophet is never accepted in his own country. People had rejected Elijah and Elisha. Now they would reject him. The furious worshipers proceeded to prove Jesus was right. Enraged they hustled him out of the synagogue and rushed him to the edge of a cliff where they threatened to throw him over and kill him. Jesus miraculously walked out of their grasping and murderous arms and walked away from his home village. So, from the very start of his ministry, the seed of opposition to his message was planted. Like the prophets of old, he would be rejected and eventually be martyred.

Begone Satan!
The Famed Capernaum Exorcism (Lk. 4:31-39)

In his desert temptations Jesus proved that Satan would not have power over him. Now Jesus liberated someone else from the domination of evil. At the Nazareth synagogue he preached the Good News of a kingdom of God that freed others from all that oppressed them, especially evil. In the Capernaum synagogue he practiced what he preached by exorcising a demon from a possessed member of the congregation.

Luke tells us that Christ's sermon that day impressed the listeners because he spoke with such authority. This meant that Jesus did more than cite other authorities as was customary. Jesus spoke with personal authority. A convinced speaker convinces others. Personal passion will ignite enthusiasm in others. Jesus sought no formal power to control others. He had no political or ecclesiastical office. He possessed no financial or military clout.

Some people crave power. They will strive to be rich, physically strong, politically eminent, famous as actors or entertainers, devious as gamblers, triumphant sexual seducers, deal makers, and other similar delusionary quests. For the most part, all they get is power, but not authority. The best these power hungry types can do is force others to comply. Their threatening, intimidating maneuvers will compel obedience, but those they scare will never internally submit.

Christ's career is a stunning reproof to all who would try to make the quest for power the road to authority. Christ's witness exposes the illusion of people who cannot understand why it turned out that the more power they had, the less authority they wielded. People will love leaders who have the courage to rely on authority. People will hate and fear those who trust on naked power alone. Power enslaves. Authority liberates. Power frightens. Authority invites loving loyalty and creative sacrifice. Power humiliates and weakens people. Authority fulfills its followers. Tyrants leave a legacy of death and destruction. Authoritative leaders produce spiritual communities that opt for life and love.

That mood of authority was communicated by Jesus in the Capernaum synagogue. After Jesus completed his sermon, the customary discussion followed. Suddenly, a discordant scream startled and shocked that little congregation. A man possessed by an unclean demon was there. The demon's cry burst from that man's mouth. It asked Jesus why he had come to destroy "them" — speaking on behalf of the community of demons.

Jesus had just spoken authoritatively to the worshipers. Now he acted with authority over the demon. With his own commanding voice he silenced the demon and demanded that it leave that poor, unfortunate man. The evil demon obeyed Christ's divine authority and exited the body of the man, throwing him in a convulsive leap from his bench to the floor in front of Christ.

The intensity and immediacy of that scene was unforgettable. No participant could be indifferent or psychologically removed — let alone physically distant — from the astounding event that day. The violent power of evil was evident. The extraordinary authority of Christ's inexhaustible goodness and love was more impressive. The mystery of love outdistanced the frightening mystery of evil. In a world where evil seemed to have too much control, a sign of liberty had appeared. Light could master darkness. Good conquered evil. Love surpassed hatred. If the participants harbored the suspicion that evil could not be overcome — only pacified — they now had reason to believe the impossible was possible.

Unlike magicians who lathered and labored to drive out demons, Jesus simply spoke with authority and drove the evil one away. Jesus used no tricks and showed no fear either of the demons nor of the opinions of those who witnessed what he was doing. In the full flow of his authority he drowned the harsh reed of evil.

This chapter of Luke concludes with the healing of Peter's mother-in-law. She was in the grip of a major fever. Jesus came to her bedside and rebuked the fever (just as he had rebuked the demon) and the fever left her. Jesus came both to conquer the cause of sickness which was sin and evil and to remove the symptom of evil which was illness. On Good Friday and Easter he would even conquer death itself — death, the ultimate outcome of evil.

In this chapter of Luke, Jesus gives us a spiritual life plan for resisting temptations. He prepares us to share our faith with others even if they reject it. And he invites us to participate with him in the removing of evil from our world. The richness of Christ's teaching, example, and grace will become even more evident as we journey with him throughout Galilee, to Jerusalem, and as we witness his redemptive actions in Holy Week and Easter time.

Reflection

1. When I am able to find some quiet time, what do I notice about the movement of my mind and imagination? If I find I am noisy inside, what can I do about it?
2. Do I feel the need for solitude in my life? What would I do with it if I had it?

3. Why should I undertake fasting for religious reasons? What would it do for me?
4. Why are prayer and meditation important for my lifelong personal change and renewal?
5. How can I come to "hear" the interior voice of the Holy Spirit? Am I afraid to be "led" by the Spirit as Christ was?
6. Jesus was not afraid to speak the truth in the Nazareth synagogue. Have there been times in my life when I fear to witness my moral beliefs for fear of rejection? Why?
7. What is the difference between a person who relies only on naked power and one who trusts in interior authority?
8. Why does the person who acts from authority help others better than one who operates from force and power?
9. What examples can I cite of a new interest in demons and diabolical possession today? What is my reaction?
10. How might Jesus be as misunderstood today as he was in his own time?

Prayer

My Jesus, you were faced with temptations and rejection just like me and all the people I know. You resisted temptation and did not fear to tell the truth even when you might be rejected. I pray that you give me that gift of spiritual character which will enable me to resist temptation and courageously witness my beliefs. Amen.

5   Called to Be a Missionary of Love

Jesus Calls His First Missionaries (Lk. 5:1-11)

Christianity is a dynamic religion. It is essentially a missionary community. It is growth oriented. Luke's gospel and his Acts of the Apostles emphasize this missionary quality of Christianity more than the other three gospels. The reader feels Luke's interest in the expansion of Christianity, its growth stretching from Jerusalem to Rome itself. His attention to the development of discipleship frequently focuses on the formation of the missionary attitude of the disciple.

At the same time, Luke avoids any type of missionary arrogance or religious imperialism. The origin and expansion of the Christian mission is always a work of divine grace. It is wrapped in the mystery of Christ's loving appeal to the human heart responding in faith.

All this is evident in Luke's first mission training story. It occurs in the context of the working lives of some fishermen. The fishing industry flourished along the shores of Galilee lake, also called Tiberias and Gennesaret. This heart shaped fresh water lake was thirteen miles long and eight miles wide. Fishing villages such as Capernaum, Bethsaida, and Magdala bordered the lake. Boats engaged in fishing and transportation sailed between the lake towns on a regular basis.

Some have speculated that the demand for carpenters for shipbuilding and maintenance may have caused Christ's change of residence from Nazareth to Capernaum. His close association with the sea made him familiar with boats, sailing, and the fishing industry.

The difference in the warm land temperatures and the cool ones in the mountains just behind the shoreline caused many sudden and violent storms. The mountains prevented the winds from touching the lake near the western beaches. Instead, the gales struck the middle of the lake and the eastern shore. Jesus encountered these storms in traveling from Capernaum to the eastern shore village of Gadara.

The fishermen used several methods to make their catch. Sometimes they employed a line with a hook on the end of it. Jesus asked Peter to catch a fish this way when he wanted to secure money to pay their taxes. "Go to the sea, drop in a hook and take the first fish that comes up. Open its mouth and you will find a coin worth twice the temple tax. Give that to them for me and for you" (Mt. 17:27).

Other times the fishermen used a broad net. They dropped the net into the water and drew it together in a narrowing circle as they pulled it into the boat, or as they dragged it toward the shore. Lastly, an individual fisherman would stand on the shore or in the shallow water and throw it into the sea in such a way that it formed a tent or a cone. Its lead weights pulled it to the bottom where it enclosed the fish. The catch was taken from this net and put in a receiving net, draped about the body of the fisherman.

The nets needed to be washed and then hung up in the sun to dry along the sides of the boats or on brushwood on the beach. The fifth chapter of Luke opens with just such a scene of fishermen washing their nets. Jesus had been preaching along the beach. The listeners crowded him as they heard God's word. Jesus asked Simon to let him use his boat as a sea-borne pulpit. That way he could teach the people from the waterside without being hemmed in by jostling crowds. This would give more people a decent chance to hear him.

Simon would have known Jesus both as a popular speaker in Capernaum and possibly as a boat builder and one capable of repairing ships. The fact that Jesus cured his mother-in-law of a fever indicates they were seemingly close friends. Their relationship was familiar enough that Jesus could ask this favor from Simon, even though his working period was over and he was cleaning his nets.

After completing his teaching, Jesus invited Simon to go back out for more fishing. Gray with fatigue and lack of sleep, Simon protested that the fishing was terrible right now. They had worked hard all through the night and caught nothing. Years of experience had taught him not to fight the odds. His practical nature prompted him to eye Jesus skeptically. He might be the best speaker the town ever heard. He was obviously a useful, skilled carpenter. He clearly needed more experience with fishing.

Jesus persisted. Simon relented and gave into what seemed to him a passing fancy. The Master would only learn from disappointing experience. Remarkably, it was Jesus who turned out to be right. Simon and his boat crew were overwhelmed by a miraculous catch of fish to the point where their nets were tearing apart. They yelled for help from their partners, James and John (sons of Zebedee), in a nearby boat. So great was the haul that both boats were in danger of sinking under the load.

The awed Simon Peter fell on his knees before Jesus and said, "Depart from me, Lord, for I am a sinful man" (verse 8). A similar religious astonishment gripped James and John. Jesus used this experience of a little miracle to invite them to participate in a far greater mystery, the missionary task of calling all peoples to accept the salvation and love offered by Jesus. Arrived back at the beach, they left everything and followed him.

Jesus called his first missionaries from a group of relatively prosperous businessmen who owned their boats and nets and came from families with a long history of successful enterprise at their local seaport. Surrendering their historic calling was not easy for them. It was not just the little miracle that changed their hearts. It was their fuller personal experience of Jesus. As leading citizens of Capernaum they would have witnessed Christ's exorcism of the demon at the synagogue.

They had listened to his preaching of the Good News many times. They had abundant opportunity to observe what kind of a man Jesus was, how he treated people and how he conducted himself. They felt his love and perceived the warmth and power that drew all kinds of people to want to press up against him (verse 1). They were not indifferent to this remarkable man whose affection touched so many, including themselves.

Against his better judgment, Simon responded to Christ's call to go back again to the sea. Basically Jesus called Simon Peter to something far deeper than a fishing expedition. But it is always through the simplicities of our daily lives that Christ calls us to the vocation of love. Jesus begins with what we know and helps us to see the hidden mystery — what we do not seem to know — buried in our regular working lives and pastimes.

Jesus dealt with Peter, James, and John in a direct and down to earth manner. He simply said that they would some day catch people instead of fish. Nothing about ambitious missionary enterprises. No glamorous visions of religious conquest. Not a word about muscular claiming of the world for Christ. Little said about mission strategies or how to achieve such a mammoth task. Just a plain line about making disciples of people, not with the same energy and practicality one searches for fish, but with trusting obedience and faith.

They would "catch people" after they were tired of working their own way all night and began working in the daytime by simply obeying Jesus in faith and trust. Their capacity to convert others would come from a source of love and grace greater than themselves. The more they relied on the energy source and strategy of divine power, the more the nets of the Christian community would be so packed with members that they would appeal to others to come and help them serve this new community.

Christ calls each one of us to be missionaries of love. Jesus appeals to us from the gifts we use to make a living and pass our time. Maybe we serve people in humble ways such as cleaning homes, making beds, working at check-out counters, or dispensing fast food. Maybe we are lawyers, counselors, bankers, developers, teachers, or entertainers. Whatever our gifts, those are the centers where Jesus summons us to be disciples of love.

The Gospel of love is the deep still point in the center of every person. Whether one is a fisherman or a financier makes little difference. Each gift is the occasion for witnessing the love of Jesus and holds the potential for being a missionary event. Ultimately, it is not what we do, but who we are. The more we are in touch with the divine center of love, the more we will radiate love to all we serve and meet.

Christ calls each of us to "leave our nets" and follow him in the sense that Jesus asks us to let go of the way our occupations dominate our lives and thoughts. Let love command our hearts and works and then we can make each task an opportunity for affection for others.

Damien Repeats Christ's Ministry to Lepers (Lk. 5:12-16)

A leper came to Jesus and asked to be healed. Jesus cured him and ordered him to show himself to a priest to receive what was substantially a bill of health. He should then make a thank-offering in the temple.

Christ's cure of the leper has inspired many of his followers to do something beautiful for God. Perhaps the greatest imitator of Christ's ministry to lepers was Father Damien of Molokai. Born in Belgium in 1840, Damien joined the missionary order of the Sacred Hearts of Jesus and Mary. Ordained at 25, he went to Hawaii as a missionary. After serving there eight years, he was missioned to the leper colony at Molokai where he spent the remaining sixteen years of his life.

He found 800 totally neglected lepers. The government gave them enough food and clothing to survive, but nothing else. The world dreaded their disease and was repulsed by its ravages. Treated as little more than animals, the lepers lived almost like them. They drank to excess and dismissed sexual and moral restraints.

The sight appalled Damien. He felt bad enough about their leprosy. The human chaos shocked him far more. He wept over their loss of human dignity and self worth. The government that kept them that way and the society that expected them to live so degradingly angered him.

Over the next sixteen years Damien shaped his beloved lepers into an orderly community. He shamed the government and the church into providing the money and supplies needed for housing, a clinic and a church building. He struggled with his people to draw them away from their lawlessness, immorality, and self-destructive behavior. He refused to let them wallow in self pity and challenged them to live up to the best Christian ideals.

Everyone resisted Damien at first — the government, the church, even the lepers. His faith, patience, and love prevailed. After eleven years he contracted leprosy but refused to leave his lepers. He rejoiced that at last he was "one of them."

Five years later, he died, leaving behind him a triumph of faith-enlightened attitudes toward the world's most unwanted people. He

performed an unusually great miracle by healing the lepers' self
hatred and replacing that with a divinely based love of self. He cured
the world's misguided expectations of lepers and introduced an enlightened attitude.

Medical science has since found a cure for leprosy or Hansen's
disease. By lifting his lepers out of a subhuman way of life and cor-
recting the world's inhuman attitudes toward them, Damien challenges all of us to have the highest reverence for the dignity of each
human being we meet. He looked beyond the leprosy to the luminous
image of God within the person. The interior beauty was greater than
the exterior disfigurement. So too, nothing must repel us in what we
behold in others, neither their physical nor moral defects. Behind it
all is the wonder of a human being waiting to be loved and transformed by our Christian affection.

Jesus Produces a "Wellness" Event (Lk. 5:17-26)

In recent years people have discovered the role of a healthy attitude in healing physical ills. They have also rediscovered the value
of regular physical exercise both for a healthy body and a positive
mental attitude. Health is the result of a total plan which repairs inner
attitudes as well as the outer body. Wellness centers (or their
equivalent) have appeared everywhere. Treatment of the full person
is better than dealing with only one side of a human being.
Moreover, preventive care lessens the need for medicinal attention.

Christ's cure of the paralytic possesses the quality of a wellness
event. The story has its enduring charm. Jesus is preaching in the interior atrium of a house. Some men arrive bearing a paralytic on a
stretcher. The packed house precludes their entering by normal
means. So they take the outside stairway to the roof, easily break a
hole in the mud and straw roof, and lower the stretcher down in front
of the amused and astonished crowd.

The scene is set for a miracle and the onlookers expect one,
given the reputation Jesus had acquired. Jesus upset their expectations by ministering to the man's spirit first of all. He told him that
his sins were forgiven. Jesus did more than address the man's
psychological attitudes or emotional feelings about himself.

The Lord probed into the heart of the paralytic and offered him spiritual and moral forgiveness. Jesus wanted to heal his soul as well as his body. The man had come to him with faith in his power to heal his body. Jesus perceived the man's faith was also open to moral healing and so he offered him this gift as well. Christ's act of forgiveness troubled the religious leaders who were present. In their minds, he had blasphemed because only God could forgive sins.

Jesus asked them if it was easier to forgive sins or heal a body. Obviously both acts are difficult. Jesus then cured the paralytic. Christ's powerful act in the observable, physical order was matched by his power over sin in the invisible, spiritual order. He showed them all a stunning example of a wellness event in the deepest sense of the word. The wellness movement today stays with the psychological and the physical. Christ would add the spiritual dimension to the psychological and physical for a complete wellness experience. Delivery from moral evil is as important for human wholeness as is liberation from emotional and physical illness.

A Tax Man's Conversion (Lk. 5:27-39)

Then Jesus went to the customs house to meet its administrator, Levi. He asked him to be a disciple. Luke notes simply that Levi (Matthew) left everything and followed Jesus. Becoming a disciple of Jesus means letting go of all that prevents one from following Christ. By participating in an unjust system of taxation, Levi belonged to the fellowship of sinners. Tax collecting and sinning meant the same thing in those times. Levi had to let go of his sinful vocation in order to follow Christ.

The scene shifts immediately from the customs house to a dining room where Levi hosted a festive meal to celebrate his conversion. Outside the Pharisees complain to Christ's disciples that it seemed scandalous to them that Jesus would eat with sinners — that is, tax men. A meal was a sign of solidarity and community. How could Jesus have solidarity with sinners? Jesus affirmed his willingness to eat with sinners. And the sinners wanted to dine with Jesus. (The solidarity fllowed both ways, from Jesus to the sinners and they to him.)

Jesus came to call sinners to repentance and conversion. A meal is a unique place for inviting sinners to conversion. Its relaxed atmosphere and its mood of loving and friendly exchange opened both the sinners to Christ's loving offer of forgiveness and Jesus himself to their moral and spiritual needs.

Some years ago the film, "Guess Who's Coming to Dinner?" showed a black man invited to a meal in a white home. The presence of a black man at a table of a white couple whose daughter was in love with him bespoke the healing of white prejudice against blacks and possibilities of reconciliation hitherto unimagined. The dining room table is a sacred place. It stands for love, acceptance, and community. It is also a setting for making such values possible.

Luke finishes his chapter with a debate about fasting and feasting. John's disciples fasted. Christ's disciples feasted. Who was right? Jesus replied that both are right in their historical context. John the Baptist's disciples represent the best in Judaism. But Christ's kingdom surpasses the old religion. Christ's disciples temporarily feast as long as he — the bridegroom — remains with them in his historical presence.

The Christian community after his resurrection and ascension will indeed fast. The situation then will be radically new. Old patches should not be sewn on this new garment. Do not try to pour old wine into this new wineskin. Put new wine into the new wineskin.

Christ has called his first missionaries. Now they will learn what it means to be his disciples and how their lives will unfold in their mission effort. Their development is a model and inspiration for our own discipleship and mission spirit.

Reflection

1. Realizing that missionaries are not only those people who go to foreign lands to convert people to Christ, how could I be a missionary in my own community?
2. How did Jesus make the miraculous catch of fish an occasion of calling Simon Peter, James, and John to be disciples?
3. What experiences in my daily life have been times when Jesus calls me to be a missionary of love?

4. In what way would I be "leaving my nets" to follow Jesus?
5. Damien looked past the visible leprosy to see the beautiful person of the leper. What stories do I have of overcoming visible traits in others in order to love and serve them?
6. What cases do I know where low expectations caused people to have a low opinion of themselves?
7. What examples can I cite of people who are committed to wellness?
8. Why should the spiritual aspect of wellness be added to the emotional and physical elements?
9. Which instances from my experience illustrate the idea that a meal is a sign of community, friendship, and love?
10. What kinds of people, if any, would I be unwilling to eat with — or be seen to dine with?

Prayer

Lord Jesus, you began your ministry by calling apostles to lead the future missionary effort of the church. Just as you called them in the daily context of their working lives, you also reach out to me in mine. Give me the grace to respond so I may become a true missionary of love.

6 Sabbath Debate and Sermon in the Valley

A mother went to her son's room to get him out of bed. "You will be late for church." Irritated, her son replied, "I don't want to go for two reasons. The people don't like me and I don't like the people." Undeterred, his mother countered, "But you must go for two reasons. First, you're the pastor and secondly, you're fifty years old."

The Sabbath Should Be Good for Your Health (Lk. 6:1-11)

Which brings us to the subject of sabbath observance, a subject of dispute between Jesus and the Pharisees. Biblical teaching insisted on two ways to observe the sabbath. First, people should rest and relax and renew themselves, hence there should be no manual labor on that day (Ex. 20:11). In this way the believers imitated God's rest on the seventh day, after working six days to make the world. Secondly, the sabbath was a day to renew one's love relationship to God by prayer and worship. That is "keeping holy" the sabbath (Dt. 5:12).

Religious laws forbade work on the sabbath such as reaping, threshing, winnowing, and preparing food. Technically, the hungry disciples broke this rule by picking a few grains in a field. They reaped a piece of grain, threshed it by rubbing it in their hands, winnowed it by throwing away the husk and "prepared" food which they ate on the sabbath.

The Pharisees grumbled to Jesus about the disciples' behavior. Jesus replied with a story about David and his companions eating the forbidden temple bread (only priests were allowed to eat it) when he was hungry. Survival needs were superior to such rules. The sabbath was made for human rest and renewal, as well as prayer and worship. It was never meant to harm persons or deprive them of essential human needs.

Luke's second sabbath story made the same point. Jesus cured a man's withered hand on the sabbath. He did this in a synagogue, the one place where the strictest observance of the sabbath should take place. The law said that doctors and healers must not work on the sabbath except to save a life or to treat eye and throat ailments. By his healing act Jesus taught that the law was never meant to forbid acts of love, kindness, caring, or mercy on the sabbath.

Enlightened rabbis held similar views, but obsessively strict ones disagreed and they controlled most sabbath custom in the majority of cases. Jesus identified himself with the more sensible rabbis, but he went much further, "The Son of Man is Lord of the sabbath" (verse 5). He would give the true meaning of sabbath. It was meant to help people focus on their relationship with God and renew themselves physically and emotionally. His position naturally angered the guardians of the law and intensified their opposition to him.

Jesus Calls His Apostles (Lk. 6:12-19)

We have already read of the call of Peter, James, John, and Matthew. Luke describes here Christ's call of all the apostles. The first calling story was in the context of a fish miracle and the mystery of faith required from those called. This second calling story is framed by prayer. Jesus went to a mountain retreat where he spent the whole night in prayer and meditation.

The selection of his apostles was one of the most important decisions of his ministry. It demanded careful thought and divine wisdom, for these apostles would become the pillars of Christianity. The fact that Jesus devoted so much time to prayer prior to his decision tells us how seriously he treated the choices and how closely the divine will was involved in it.

He did not pick perfect candidates, but people with a mixture of talents and flaws, gifts and frailties. They were pilgrims, not saints. They represented a range of human foolishness: vanity, ambition, jealousy, cowardice, doubt, bravado, betrayal, and overreaching.

Still, in the end, they proved to be made of the stuff of saints. The Holy Spirit led them to be loving, truthful, brave, loyal, assured, humble, and saintly. Most of them witnessed Christ even to the point of martyrdom. Only one of them failed Christ's expectations.

The Sermon on the Plain—
The Four Sources of Christian Happiness (Lk. 6:20-26)

The best known of Christ's sermons is the Sermon on the Mount in Matthew, chapters 5-7. Actually, that is a collection of Christ's wise teachings about covenant love and moral guidelines taken from the numerous sermons he preached and put in one place in an orderly arrangement.

To a great extent the Sermon on the Mount was Christ's explanation of the ten commandments, which he interpreted in the light of covenant love between God and the people. He broke open each commandment's spiritual meaning and showed his listeners what inner love attitude made it possible to fulfill the purpose of the commandment. Fidelity forestalls adultery. Love makes the world safe for life. Community trust protects property. Truth makes people free.

Luke provides a much shorter version of Matthew's account in his Sermon on the Plain. In Matthew, Jesus gives his sermon on a mountain, like Moses giving the law from Sinai. In Luke, Jesus gives his sermon in a valley, like a friend who says he is our support in life's daily struggle.

At Sinai, God first invited the people to a union of love. The divine-human love affair is the best assurance of human happiness. Only then did he entrust to them the commandments that showed them how to stay in love with him. In both Matthew and Luke, Jesus began his sermon with a love song called "The Beatitudes," a description of the sources of human happiness. The melody is the same in both gospels. Though the approach differs, Jesus outlines in both cases his Christian dream of love which says that permanent human happiness always includes union with God. All the rules that follow are simply ways to stay in love with self, others, and God.

In Luke's account, Jesus spoke of four sources of happiness: poverty of spirit, a hunger for God, the gift of grieving, and the positive uses of rejection. Each source deserves a brief reflection.

(1) *Poverty of Spirit.* Jesus said the poor in spirit are happy because they experience the kingdom of Heaven. People who are too filled with themselves (the "rich") miss this joy. Material poverty is simply a symbol of spiritual poverty. Whether we are actually materially poor, or ranked among the rich and famous, our true and lasting happiness comes only from spiritual poverty.

The only people who experience this are those who have an awareness of their inner life. Those who take a journey within the self will one day arrive at a boundary they cannot seem to cross. Like a jogger who hits a "wall" and believes he or she cannot go further, inner searchers also run up against a frustrating block. No political power, muscular strength, or fat bank accounts help here. The person may be as brilliant as Einstein, ingenious as Michelangelo or logical as Aristotle. None of these talents can move the person through the inside wall. Brains and money falter at this inner boundary.

Only poverty of spirit will move us through it. This is the poverty that moves us to acknowledge we have no resources of our own to go further. We will not like this challenge. It will makes us feel hostile, stubborn, and uneasy. It is hard to stop being god. We must confront ourselves as honestly as we ever did before.

No one wants to abandon the illusion that we are presumably independent of God. Even ostensibly religious people. Especially those who bravely set out on the hero journey of faith. Even though circumstances may force us to depend on others in this world, we live by the myth that we can make it on our own in the inner journey. Religious as we think we are, we bristle at depending on God. After all, should not adults be self determining?

In this sacred space — our personal inner limit — Christ offers us the cross. Jesus asks us to accept our own finiteness, our boundary, our limit. He is not trying to make us feel inadequate nor is he "putting us in our place." Jesus is excited that we have come to the turn in the road where we could begin to experience resurrection. All we need to do is stretch out our hesitant hands of faith and honestly pick up our limits, own them, rest in dependence on the Lord, and wait for the miracle of divine response. That is when Jesus takes us across the river of death and into the kingdom of resurrection. Then we lose our own limits and walls. Because of Jesus we walk in a free, bigger inner world. Jesus enriches our consciousness with happiness and surprising new strength.

(2) *Hunger for God.* The second source of happiness is hunger for God. Those who empty themselves with self preoccupations will be filled with Christ's happiness. Those who are too filled with themselves will feel spiritually empty. Most people pass their days satisfying their various hungers. Some of this is legitimate and necessary, such as taking care of one's family, health, and needs for a decent way of life.

But as one's inner life develops, there are hungers that should be let go so that one may be empty enough to be filled with God. What are some of these passionate desires? Some invest their hopes of self-fulfillment totally in their career and profession. Some crave recognition from peers and employers. Others collect affirmation to the point where no amount of it is enough. A few are sympathy gatherers, adopting a mournful face and slumped shoulders to obtain a deluge of solicited compassion.

Now it is healthy for a person to have received a reasonable measure of self fulfillment, recognition, affirmation, and sympathy. The problem arises when the person hungers too much for such satisfactions and wants to fill up the self with these daily strokes. Jesus noted that the people who are "rich" with such fillings are spiritually empty. Only when they are willing to let go of such longings will they feel a hunger for God and lasting love. Only when the native human appetite is redirected away from self and toward the Holy Spirit of love, can there be a filling of the soul by divine and permanent satisfaction. We get what we hunger for. If we hunger for what will make empty, that is what happens. If we hunger for lasting love, we will receive it.

(3) *The Grieving Shall Laugh.* The poet Robert Bly says that real humans grieve. He conducts human development seminars for men whose personal growth was stunted by growing up in a home without a father (either due to divorce or the father was "married" to his job) and who lacked a male mentor to guide them in the ways of the adult world. Bly contends that one of his chief tasks is to help grown men to grieve. Mourning is a healing event in the face of per-

sonal loss due either to death or some tragedy. A good cry will generate a good laugh. In the night of sorrow we sow our tears. Then we rejoice in the dawn.

Jesus agrees as he cites his third source of happiness. "Blessed are you who are now weeping, for you will laugh" (verse 21). Jesus took this well known fact about grief and applied it to the development of spiritual happiness. Our inner journey is a process of letting go. We shed a lot of heavy baggage. Each time we let go there is a jolt, a small death of loss and pain. We cannot help grieving for this, but the outcome causes us new joy.

The biblical Abraham left home, let go of friends, familiar surroundings and all those cultural ties that meant so much to him. He left the warm, familiar surroundings of his home. It is not hard to see the tears on his face. He grieved. The biblical narrative shows him going through many more wrenching separations. Yet after the tears, Abraham found joy. His is the experience of the psalmist, "Although they go forth weeping ... they shall come back rejoicing" (Ps. 126:6). This has to be done in faith. Abraham's faith grew so deeply that he is still celebrated as the father of faith thousands of years later.

We have the same call. We may not like leaving the "home" of those aspects of self that diminish our ability to love and believe. The prospect of grieving distresses us. Yet the results are worth the effort. Who does not like a hearty laugh? All the faith journeys in the Bible and church history tell us how effective this process is. Jesus wants us to be happy even when he cautions us, "First, you cry."

(4) *Let People Reject You.* Christ's fourth source of happiness is acceptance of rejection when it occurs because we stand up for him. It has often been said we live in the "post-Christian era." This means that the standards of the cultures where Christianity was once a dominant force no longer prevail. Some speak of the new cultural standards as those of secular humanism. Whatever the term, the reality is here.

A disciple of Christ today will often need to be countercultural. The disciple risks being rejected and insulted because of this, but will come away from the experience with soul intact and integrity preserved. In the English Reformation, Cardinal Wolsey compromised his principles in dealing with King Henry VIII, only to have the king betray him in the end. In his final moment of truth, he said, "Had I but served my God with half the zeal I served my king, he would not in mine age have left me naked to mine enemies" (*Henry the Eighth*, Act 3, Scene 2).

Our post-Christian culture can cause our Christianity to be watered down with a series of small compromises. Like Chinese water torture, each drop of water (read compromise) wears a hole in the rock of our faith in Christ. Loss of the good opinion of others scares us. Popular acclaim means too much to us. We abandon our hero journey. Like fish we swallow the hook, line and lead sinker of popular approval. We wriggle helplessly, mouth open, for a few more crumbs of fame and fortune. It is never enough and it never satisfies.

Yet Jesus patiently invites us to real happiness. To be despised for being morally courageous far outweighs craven compromise with an anti-Christian standard. To be insulted for standing up for the cause of love surpasses praise for supporting self-destructive behavior. To be denounced for loving Jesus will do more good for people than collaborating with those who dismiss Jesus, his church, and his teachings.

Covenant Applications (Lk. 6:27-49)

After Jesus delivered his vision for human happiness, he set forth applications of his covenant dream. He presented four memorable guidelines.

(1) *Live by the Golden Rule*. "Do unto others as you would have them do unto you" (verse 31). Learning to love expands when the person treats others the way one wants to be treated. If I want respect, understanding, affection, and appreciation, then I will be respectful, understanding, affectionate, and appreciative of others. A wise old priest on his eighty-sixth birthday told his friends, "I have two lessons from my life to pass onto you. First, remember the only thing that really counts in life is doing some good for another person. Secondly, never forget that someone always needs you."

Jesus further stated that love means doing good to people that hate us, praying for those who persecute us and blessing those who curse us.

(2) *Confront your own faults.* Jesus cautions us to stop concentrating on other people's faults. This causes us to condemn them, gossip about them, place them in an inferior position to ourselves. It is better to approach the sins of others with forgiveness. The more forgiving we are to others, the more we will be forgiven our own sins. Looking at other people's defects is usually an excuse to ignore our own shortcomings. We should take the log out of our own eye before trying to remove the splinter in someone else's.

(3) *Strive to have a good heart.* A bad tree produces rotten fruit. A bad person will yield misery for everyone. Pay attention to the condition of your heart, opening it to love and goodness. Then there will be acts that witness creative, life-giving behavior.

(4) *Build your life on a rock.* Those who listen to Jesus and draw power from his four sources of happiness will be like people who build houses on rock that withstand the storms of life. Those who fail to do so will build their lives on superficial sand. When the storms of life come, they will be swept away.

Christ's Sermon on the Plain speaks to the condition of our inner selves. He offers us a four-point formula for happiness and four attitudes for loving behavior. He is resolutely spiritual in his advice. Jesus does want to change our behavior, but chooses a transformation of our inner lives to bring that about. These powerful tools for inner change have never been expressed more clearly. Now it is our turn to render the "yes" of faith.

Reflection

1. How do I observe the Christian Sabbath, that is, Sunday?
2. How could I best make Sunday a day of relaxation, personal renewal, worship, and prayer?
3. What does Jesus mean when he says the Sabbath was made for people, not people for the Sabbath?
4. How would I explain poverty of spirit to myself or to a friend?
5. Since I know that self-fulfillment is a value for me, how can Jesus ask me to let go of this hunger? What does he mean?
6. Why do people need to be helped to grieve? Why is it said that men have difficulty grieving? Why does Jesus use this truth

about grieving to say that it leads to "laughter?"

7. What are some experiences in my life where I needed to stand up for my belief in Christ and his message and endure painful opposition because of it?

8. What are some cases I know of where people refuse to forgive each other? How would I help people pray for their enemies, bless those that curse them and love those who mistreat them?

9. Share success stories that illustrate the Golden Rule.

10. What are some techniques for turning away from attention to other people's faults and looking at the defects in one's own soul?

Prayer

Jesus, source of all true happiness, open me to receive your four gifts of joy in Luke's account of the beatitudes. Awaken me to the reality of my inner life and lead me on the journey to a loving union with you. Help me to embrace your gifts for powerful personal change. Transform my heart with your love.

7   A Soldier, a Widow, and a Sinful Woman

The Faith of a Soldier (Lk. 7:1-10)

A mountain climber, nearing his goal, suddenly slipped and found himself at the end of his rope, swinging fatefully between heaven and earth. He cried out, "Is there anyone up there?" God answered, "Yes." "Can you help me?" asked the worried man. "Yes I can," said God. "Let go!" Swaying doubtfully over the silent abyss, the man cried out, "Is there anyone else up there?"

Religious faith is a humble and trusting surrender to the strength of God. Solid faith is a habit of the heart. A habit results from repeated actions over a very long period of time and after many failures. A person can believe, but when tested, collapses into doubt and fear because faith is not yet grooved into his or her heart.

In a dentist's chair I can believe the novocaine will work, but relapse into panic and fear that it will not. A woman may know that her boyfriend just cannot keep a confidence, but once she is with him and filled with the warmth of the encounter, she will often ignore her belief and tell him things she wished she had kept to herself. Americans pride themselves on their scientific practicality, yet many will pay expensive astrologers to advise them on business decisions and travel plans.

Sticking to what one believes is difficult whether one's faith is in science or religion. Christian faith is personal trust in Jesus. It needs practice, just as trying to hit a tennis ball properly needs repeated tries. The humility and trust, so essential to a faith act, are not acquired easily. Only when we bounce back from constant failures do we really begin to believe in a stable and continuous way.

The story of the Roman solider who had faith in Christ is a remarkable model of a man who had the habit of faith. In many ways he had all those modern qualities that are supposed to make religious faith impossible in these secular times.

(1) *He was a professional*. As a centurion, he was in charge of one hundred men. He had chosen the military as his career and was given a promotion with important responsibilities. He had proven himself and was climbing the ladder of military rank. Many of today's professionals often think that their education and rational mastery of their fields leave little time for religious faith growth. Unspoken is the assumption that there might be something "unprofessional" about faith.

(2) *He was civic minded*. Responsive to imperial policy which sought to pacify subjugated peoples by supporting their religious practices in return for cooperation, he had built a synagogue in Capernaum. As far as the government was concerned this was simply a way to keep the peace and siphon off hostile feelings in the conquered peoples. It was cheap enough to build a religious shrine so long as it purchased conformity. Some civic minded leaders today will often do the same because it is good for business or community relations, not necessarily because they have any use for religion as such.

(3) *He used his authority*. The centurion had authority and was not afraid to use it. He ran a tight ship. He expected his orders to be obeyed. Yet power corrupts and absolute power corrupts absolutely. Modern high rollers speak of power suits and power lunches. The quest for power through money fulfills the old adage, "He who controls the gold, controls." Power seekers dismiss religion as irrelevant to their more important concerns.

Happily, the centurion did not let his professionalism, civic mindedness or personal authority prevent him from having true religious faith. His competency as a soldier did not obscure his taste for an inner spiritual life. When he built a synagogue for the Jews, he did it out of affection for them. "He loves our nation" (verse 5). He exercised his power with a sense of moral responsibility, not just for ego-strokes.

Above all he treated his slave as a person, not a thing to be used, abused and thrown away as his culture taught him. We see in him a man of unusual depth. He sensed the mystery of Jesus, not just as a miracle worker, but a kindred spiritual person. He sent Jewish elders to ask Jesus to save the life of his slave. The elders vouched for the centurion's exceptional personal integrity and strongly urged Jesus to help.

Jesus agreed and went straight to the soldier's house. But before he could reach it, the soldier intercepted him. He knew that Jewish religious custom balked at entering the home of a gentile. He would not want to test the religious sensitivities of Jesus. He said that he was not worthy to have such a wonderful person enter his home. Using his own experience of command and control in the military order, he believed Jesus had a similar power in the spiritual order.

Humbly and simply, he asked Jesus merely to say a healing word and his slave would be cured. The soldier amazed Jesus who turned to the crowd and said he had not found faith like this among his own people. He cured the slave "from a distance," just as the centurion requested.

Luke does not say how the soldier acquired such deep faith, but it is certain that he obtained the habit by long practice and persistence. That is the path we need to travel as well.

The Widow Wept and Laughed (Lk. 7:11-17)

Intense sorrow caused by death can either be bottled up or released. If the sorrow is repressed, the person may seethe with anger at the injustice of death, or seek the route of self pity. Mourning customs deal with that ache that might otherwise be self destructive.

Modern Jewish people practice "Sitting Shiva." This is a mourning period of eight days after the swift burial of the beloved. The immediate family stays at home, while friends and relatives come by to visit, prepare food and take care of the house. The presence of so many people helps the bereaved to express their sorrow, weep without shame and receive consoling embraces and handshakes.

Much the same reason stands behind the custom of waking the body. The gathering of friends, the expressions of sympathy, the urging of the bereaved to meet friends and talk and cry are meant to release pent up feelings in an approved and acceptable fashion. Spiritual people sometimes speak of the "gift of tears." What they mean is that emotional relief that comes from a good cry is indeed a gift from God.

After Jesus saved the centurion's slave from death's door, he traveled to the village of Naim. He encountered a funeral procession outside the gates of the town. The dead person was a young man, the only son of his widowed mother. The intense grief of the mother and the tears of the mourners moved Jesus to the depths of his heart.

The great English statesman Edmund Burke has said, "Next to love, sympathy is the divinest passion of the human heart." The capacity to grieve is one of our most human sentiments. So often Jesus is presented in abstract theological terms. Frequently, his humanity drowns in a declamation about his divine qualities or his ethical teachings. People often present him either as a cold deity or a university ethics professor.

Scripture does not avoid naming Christ's transcendent, heavenly origins nor his demanding moral teachings. But the Bible also asks us to look at his endearing human qualities. Luke invites us to gaze at Jesus meeting perfect strangers at a funeral, encountering a heartbroken widow crying over her deceased only son. Look at Jesus melting with sorrow, showing his grief, exposing his heart to people he has never met before.

This was not just another funeral to him. He did not steel his heart against the sorrow and pity of the widow. He did not avert his eyes or whisper to his apostles to hurry past this "distracting" scene in an attitude of studied indifference. Nor did he choose a formal exterior gravity, a polite nod to local custom that would exonerate him from a human connection to the event.

No, Jesus grieved. The sound of tears hit a chord in his own heart. The sight of a lonely widow touched him. He let himself be affected. He could feel the emotions of sadness and sympathy. We see in him how God would act in that scene. Jesus went to the widow and held her saying, "Do not weep" (verse 13). Then he confronted the mystery of death, an evil that he had resolved to overcome. He raised the young man from the dead. The man rose and began to speak. Jesus united the son with his amazed and ecstatic mother.

Our contemporary culture is nervous about death. It teaches us to deny its reality and counsels males especially to hide their grief.

Jesus shows us that facing death is better than denying it and grieving is necessary and valuable. Our faith tells us that Jesus has conquered death and that it is not the end, but a transition into eternal love and happiness.

John the Baptist's Mission (Lk. 7:18-35)

In Luke 3:20, we saw that Herod had imprisoned John the Baptist for speaking out against his unlawful and immoral marriage. Now Luke tells us that the Baptist's disciples came to him and told him of the successes of Jesus. Strangely, the Baptist sent them to Jesus to ask if he really is the messiah, the "one who is to come." Why would the prophet whose whole mission was to announce the messiah, who had in fact baptized him at the Jordan, who knew him as a cousin now seem to express doubts about Jesus?

Some commentators argue that John's faith was assured, but he wanted Jesus to reassure his disciples personally.

Others suggest that the anguish of his imprisonment, the dark night of his soul, the physical confinement of a man used to the freedom of the desert caused him to ache for affirmation. Severe tests mark the faith journey of any person, above all for those who have great spiritual gifts such as the Baptist possessed. He would not be immune to the trials of the inner night of faith.

Jesus advised the disciples to return to John and tell him of his works and his teachings. Christ's personal witness, miracles, and words revealed his identity. This did not "prove" Christ's messiahship in a rational and logical way. It was evidence that asked the beholder to respond in faith. The prison shrouded the Baptist in the mystery of its own darkness. Even so esteemed a prophet as John would be challenged to respond in faith to the evidence Jesus sent him.

He would also hear that Jesus praised him as the greatest man ever born of woman, meaning he was the greatest prophet of the first covenant. Then the disciples would tell him that Jesus said the least in the kingdom — the new covenant — would be greater than he. This meant that a child of grace born into the Christian covenant began at a new and richer spiritual level because of the graces available from Christ.

Finally, the disciples told John how much Jesus praised his prophetic ministry. Jesus had glowingly spoken of the missionary strength of his cousin. John was no reed shaken by the wind, not a court prophet that preached the fashions of the hour and stroked the smugness of the people, not a man who measured his sermons by the polls. Nor was he a soft "kept man" dressing luxuriously and eating at the best tables, associating only with the rich and famous. Rising to his point Jesus declared that John was a real prophet, the greatest that Israel had ever heard.

Hence, while Jesus asked faith from his cousin, he was not without human sympathy for his suffering in the jail. Jesus knew that John needed affirmation and provided him with a powerful dose of it. His rousing defense of John's ministry was an affectionate and profound support for his dear friend. Lest John had any doubt about what Jesus thought of his work, it was now clear that Jesus had nothing but the highest respect for it.

Lastly, Jesus noted that the problem was not with his preaching or that of John. This was not a case of religious rivalry. The difficulty lay in the hearts of the listeners. They were still playing games like children who tease one another with mock funerals and weddings. A child played a flute as if leading a wedding dance and the other kids would refuse to dance, or another child would sing a funeral chant and the playmates would not cry. His message and that of John both required openness to God's love and grace.

Instead many of them called John a "demon" for fasting from feasts and rejecting wine. And they called Jesus a glutton for eating good meals and drinking wine with sinners. Christianity is more than a game for dismissing a saving message with cheap shots. Only faith filled wisdom would help people overcome this superficial way of treating a message that offers them the only real happiness that lasts.

The Woman Who Loved Jesus (Lk. 7:36-50)

A pharisee named Simon invited Jesus to dinner. He omitted the usual courtesies due a guest. Jesus expected a formal kiss of greeting, water to rinse the dust from his feet and a few drops of perfume (often the essence of rose petals) sprinkled on his head. Even the poorest family would host a guest this way. No such politeness was given to Jesus. In today's terms this would be like arriving at a host's home for a dinner, receiving no handshake or hug, being left to hang up one's coat on one's own and hearing no warm words of the perfume of welcome. Such was the cold reception Jesus received.

A sinful woman of the city learned that Jesus was in Simon's home. The context of the story implies that the woman was a prostitute. Unannounced, she intruded upon the dinner party, shocking everyone there by her unwanted presence. Given her reputation, she wounded the sensibilities of the seated guardians of public morality. She offended their sense of propriety by approaching Jesus, kneeling before him, shedding tears on his feet, rubbing them with the water from her eyes and kissing them with her lips. She dried them with her hair. She brought an expensive alabaster phial of perfume, all of which she emptied upon his feet, anointing them with its fragrance.

Simon and his companions could not believe their eyes. Why was Jesus allowing her to do this? Why did he not pull away in disgust or order the servants to have her expelled? How could he let this moral untouchable place her hands on his feet and kiss them?

The overpowering sweetness of a whole bottle of fragrance poured out with abandon did not sweeten their attitudes, but had the opposite effect of souring their feelings. She had polluted their moralistic environment with her "evil" presence. As one of the town's most socially disapproved persons, she had filled the home of a religious leader with the taint of scandal. It was difficult to tell what bothered them more — the presence of a sinner or simply that of a social pariah.

The only one who did not look upset with her was Jesus. He smiled at her and made her feel welcome and at home. If Jesus was discontent with anyone it was with his hosts and he let them know it. He did not confront them with a public criticism at first, but rather with a story about a creditor. One person owed him a large sum of money and the other a small amount. The creditor forgave both debts. Which one would love him more? Simon replied that the one with the big debt would feel the most love and gratitude.

Jesus agreed and proceeded to contrast their discourteous treatment of him with the affectionate treatment he received from the woman. Detail by detail, Jesus forthrightly compared their callousness with the woman's kindness. Then he lifted the conversation to the moral level they loved so well. He turned matters upside down.

They dwelt hypocritically on her sins. Jesus focused on her faith and love. They viewed her from a harsh lack of compassion and forgiveness. He saw her as a woman who had the potential for great love and personal conversion. They saw in her only moral ugliness. Jesus saw more, her inner hunger for love and forgiveness, her potential for spiritual transformation. This theme was later captured by the musical play, "The Man of La Mancha," in which La Mancha sees the goodness in the prostitute, Aldonza. He gives her a new vision of herself by renaming her Dulcinea, singing to her that her name "is like a prayer an angel whispers."

Jesus told the dinner guests that the woman's great sins have been forgiven because she has loved much and she has believed it was possible. Looking at her with the most profound love, Jesus said, "Your faith has saved you. Go in peace" (verse 50). We never get to know the woman's name. In a sense she stands for Everyman and Everywoman — for all of us who need to learn we can be changed, transformed from sinner into one who is forgiven.

Love surrounds the whole transformation event. Love brought her to Jesus. Jesus brings her to greater love. Jesus tried to loosen up those tight-minded religious leaders. He hoped to warm their hearts and set them free. He succeeded with a detested sinner. The defenders of religion stonewalled him. The question today is not what they did. The event questions our consciences now. What will we do?

Reflection

1. The centurion's professionalism, civic mindedness, and authority could have inhibited his faith growth but did not. How could these traits stall our faith growth?
2. The soldier knew how to be humble. How can we acquire the humility that goes with true faith? What is the difference between humility and unwholesome self abasement?
3. Grieving is important when there is an occasion that demands it.

What are some stories I know of where people seemed unable to grieve when they should have?

4. Why do males, as a rule, find it harder to grieve than females?
5. When Jesus grieved with the widow of Naim, what did he show us about his humanity?
6. What do I think is the real reason John the Baptist sent disciples to Jesus to ask whether or not he was the messiah?
7. What did Jesus mean when he said the Baptist was the greatest man born of woman, but the least in the kingdom is greater than he?
8. Why did Jesus make such a point of lavishly praising John?
9. Do I have stories where I was treated shabbily as a guest in someone else's home?
10. What makes this forgiveness story of the sinful woman so memorable?

Prayer

Jesus, you cured the slave of the centurion, resurrected the son of the widow of Naim, and forgave a sinful woman. Touch me with the transforming love you exercised in these three events. Move me to be open to your presence and change me into a vital witness of your love.

8   Faith Responses and Life Stages

Once upon a time a turtle and a scorpion came to the bank of a swollen river. The scorpion begged the turtle to ferry him across those rushing waters. The turtle refused. "No, I won't take you because you will sting me on the neck with your poison." "Why would I do that," replied the scorpion. "You are my life raft. If I stung you, we would both drown." The turtle believed the scorpion. "Well, since you put it that way, I guess it's all right. Climb aboard."

The scorpion jumped on the turtle's back and they moved to the middle of the river. At that moment the scorpion stung the turtle and they both began to sink in the torrent. The turtle said to the scorpion, "Before we drown I have to know why you did this to me." Somewhat embarrassed, the scorpion confessed, "I really don't know. What can I say? I just couldn't help myself. It's my nature."

This story is a parable about the puzzling destructive behavior of human beings, even when they know better. People of all cultures have invented stories and parables to illustrate truths about human nature. Teachers, preachers, playwrights, and poets have all resorted to the parable to put across a point. They instinctively knew that an appeal to the imagination captures attention better than abstract statements. They understood that stories are rich tools for understanding human mystery and religious mystery as well.

In the art of the parable, no one has surpassed the skill of Jesus. So expertly did he fashion his parables that they have become the most memorable forms of all his teachings, even among people who have little contact with religion.

A Farmer and a Lamp (Lk. 8: 1-21)

After noting that a community of women accompanied Jesus and the apostles on the preaching journeys (they provided financial assistance for the mission), Luke launches into a report of the first two parables Jesus preached.

Luke begins with Christ's parable of a farmer sowing his seed with varying degrees of effectiveness. A lot depended on the receptivity of the ground. Drop it on a footpath whose soil is packed from people walking on it and see the seed resting on top of the ground and waiting for birds to come and feast on it. Throw it among thorns and note that the brambles choke it from growing. Scatter the seed on rocks and expect it to wither because there is no moisture. Sow it in good ground and be assured it will take root and produce a crop.

In that rural culture, Christ could assume his listeners were perfectly familiar with the agricultural story he had told. Jesus proceeded to apply it to the preaching of the Word of God. The seed was the Word. The various kinds of ground were the differing human responses to Christ's invitation to love and acceptance of salvation.

Jesus emphasized in this parable the human reaction to his call to love. He fully appreciated that whatever is received is taken in according to the capacity of the receiver. The dispositions of the heart modify the ability to receive salvation.

Contemporary thinking views such a capacity in terms of stages of faith development. While a human response is always more complex than a stage implies, it is useful to see it this way. Generally speaking one can speak of the receptivity of a person from the teenage years onward in the following way.

(1) *Teenage Years (13-19) — the Rocky Ground.* The adolescent has begun to discover a sense of self. Relationships become intensely important because one person reveals to the other this sense of self. As someone has put it, "I see you seeing me. The me I see is the one I think you see." This accounts for the crushes and emotional involvement which happens at this stage. The delight of discovery depends on the other, hence I must cling to that person in order to cling to "me." In this period the person of Jesus will seem very attractive to the teenager.

The parish that provides a strong community for youth and a personal approach to Christ, doctrine, and the institution will appeal to the teenager at this level. However, this is "rocky soil," for the youth tend to receive Christ with enthusiastic joy, but often without a careful rooting of the relationship. They believe for a while and then drift away especially when the moral challenges of the Gospel become too much for them.

(2) *Young Adults (20- 40) — the Foot Path.* The young adults move beyond the emotional involvements of the adolescent years into a lively rational approach to life. Instead of depending on others for self discovery, the young adult is an independent minded self starter. Whereas a personal approach to Jesus was all important in the previous years, now an intellectual focus seems more attractive. There is a move from feelings to logic.

The parish that provides a chance for young adults to get involved with the church in its liturgical planning and decision making will appeal to the young adults. A parish that has adult religious education — either for home renewal groups or for parish center reflection — will respond to the religious intellectual needs of such members.

The main problem here is precisely the emphasis on logic to the exclusion of the religion of the heart. This is the "foot path" problem. Jesus says these people have heard God's Word but the devil (the birds of the air) comes and takes it away. Logic alone is too narrow a soil for religious penetration. It is open only to the air, the sun, and the rain. But without a heart in which to sink love into the earth of one's soul, it stays on one level where it is gobbled up by the disputatious "birds of the air," those who make theology a mind game and forget the other side of religion.

(3) *Mid-life Adult (40-55) — the Thorns.* The first autumn leaves are falling. Premonitions of death begin. The person still feels young but also senses growing old. Emotions and logic are valued but neither are seen in an exaggerated state that earlier stages provided. The mid-life adult is more patient with paradox, with the seeming contradictions of life. Things are not so simple as they once seemed. A sense of life's mystery settles in, causing a forgiving attitude toward people and life's bumpy road.

Parish prayer groups, meditation, adoration of the Blessed Sacrament and other forms of popular religion will have a growing appeal to mid-life adults. For many of them this is the beginning of the "spiritual phase" of their lives. Divine realities do not seem so overpowering, far from it, they appear to be the liberating forces that they have always claimed to be.

The pitfall here is the mid-life crisis. Instead of going with the flow, many regress to the rampant emotionalism of early youth or the rigid rationalism of the first years of young adulthood. This is both a form of death denial and a refusal to accept the fact of aging. These are the Peter Pan's who both hate growing up and growing old. In Christ's words these people are choked by the thorns of life, its anxieties, riches, and pleasures. Financially they are usually well enough off to finally "enjoy" life and its pleasures. The anxieties attendant on wrinkles and graying suffocate them, so they regress with artificial means. They cannot feel Christ calling them now because they want to live in a world of illusions.

(4) *Seniors (55 and Beyond) — The Good Ground.* Those who have grown old gracefully will grow in grace. They no longer cling to their ego's because they are discovering another "I" — that of Jesus Christ. That is what St. Paul meant when he said, "I live, no longer I, but Christ lives in me" (Gal. 2:20). This is a deep and mysterious exchange known only to those who persevere in their inner journey and come to see the ease and freedom that comes from having Christ as the center of one's life.

They are the living reminders of the "good ground" of which Jesus spoke. They have heard Christ's word, embraced it with a generous and good heart and persevered to the point where that word is the love that shapes their beliefs, attitudes, and practices. They are the beautiful people of our families, parishes, and civic communities. Quietly, they live and move and have their being in Christ. They are the living saints who witness for us what Christianity is all about. Their modesty and unassuming ways make them seem more like an aura, a light that enfolds others silently and encourages them to the life of love and forgiveness in which ultimate happiness is finally found.

This "stage theory " interpretation of Christ's parable of the Sower, must be taken for what it is worth. It is a general picture of human and spiritual growth, for which there are many exceptions. An individual Christian is rarely found in the pure state of one of the stages.

Nor do people parade through life in exact footwork to the sound of these drums. A young teenager, like Thérèse of Lisieux, was already at the spiritual level of the senior people described in this staging chart. Some never seem to grow up. Others advance rapidly on the mysterious path of faith. There are two mysteries at work, that of the Holy Spirit's influence and that of the human person. It is exactly this twofold mystery that takes the predictability out of the progression.

The parable of the Sower is a picture of what Pope John Paul II calls the "dialogue of salvation." Like a dance, the divine and human partners advance, retreat, unite, separate, seemingly part forever, and then miraculously return, clasping each other in an embrace of love that is splendidly fulfilling. No other relationship available to a human being surpasses this inner drama. A good marriage exhibits what it might be like. A lifelong, tender friendship hints at its possibilities. Love triumphant in any experience is an echo of this inner journey. The peace that results surpasses all understanding because it is not based on logic alone. The love that evolves seems like the most original that ever existed. Why? Because it comes from the Holy Spirit, the very originator of love itself.

Our Lamp of Faith Is Our Sharing of Love

Jesus adds the parable of the lamp to his discussion of the sower. Having shown the impracticality of hiding a lamp under the bed, he says the lamp of our faith must be visible to all to see and enjoy. It has been said that only two percent of Catholics are willing to share their faith with others. American Catholics have bought the idea that religion is a private affair, a matter of one's own conscience, nobody else's business. Jesus does not agree. There is no right to privacy when it comes to sharing the Good News of love.

Jesus says that faith and love are essentially united. Love is faith's public expression. We cannot truly have faith without also loving self, others, and God. To hide faith is to hide love and to deny to other people the joy and hope that faith in Christ provides. This does not mean we should force our love and faith on others. We are not talking about church imperialism. Love that is forced is not love.

That is a smothering of the other. Love and faith demand freedom of acceptance.

We are talking about love's responsibility once it has been received. If Jesus has loved and forgiven us, should we not share that Good News with others? Sharing is invitational, affectionate, attracting. To let our lamp of faith shine is to let others know in a gentle and winning way how great is the gift we have received from Jesus. When Christ's family came to see him and could not reach him, Jesus pointed to his own mother and relatives — whom he loved dearly — as an example of what he was driving at. Faith is "family producing." It is not a private matter. Those who hear God's Word and accept it are members of the loving family of Jesus. Our lamps must shine and share.

Jesus Calms a Storm (Lk. 8:22-25)

Jesus and the apostles were sailing across Galilee to Gerasa when a sudden storm arose. Jesus was asleep. The apostles woke him up alerting him to the danger. Jesus calmed the storm and rebuked them for their lack of faith in the midst of life's storms. The following story is one way of appreciating this event.

After heavy rain a flood began. A stubborn man sat on a rocker on his porch watching a rowboat go by. The occupants of the rowboat invited the man to climb in but he refused saying, "God will take care of me." The next day the flood waters rose to the second floor of the man's home. A motor launch appeared at his window to rescue him. The man clutched his bible to his heart and said he was trusting in God alone. The third day, the man sat on his roof as the waters surged angrily about him. A helicopter hovered over him with a rescue rope. The man raised his hands to heaven and said, "The Lord is my shepherd." The man drowned the next day and went to heaven. He protested to God, "You let me down. I trusted in you." But God replied, "But I tried to save you three times."

Jesus Exorcises the Gerasene Demoniac (Lk. 8:26-39)

Gerasa is on the eastern shore of Galilee. It is in the territory often called "Galilee of the Gentiles." On the Gerasa beach Jesus met a man possessed by demons. The tormented man wore no clothes, refused to live in a house, and slept in a cemetery. When he was thought to be a threat to the villagers, strong armed men captured him and bound him in chains, to no avail, for he snapped the bonds and walked away. Jesus began to exorcise the devil from the man. Addressing Jesus as "Son of the most high God," a voice spoke through the man begging Jesus to stop the process. Jesus asked the name of the demon, who replied, "Legion."

Jesus saw a herd of swine nearby and expelled the demons from the man. The demons went into the pigs. The herd rushed to the lake and drowned. The event frightened the townspeople, who asked Jesus to leave them. The healed man thanked Jesus and asked to join his band of disciples. Jesus commissioned him instead to be an evangelist to his own people, telling them the story of what God had done for him.

Even for Christian believers in exorcism, the story has several puzzling aspects. Why would Jesus destroy a herd of pigs? Was that not unfair to their owner and prejudicial to his livelihood? No satisfactory answer can be given. Some believe this was a legendary, comic detail added to amuse the Jewish listeners who were forbidden to eat pork or raise pigs. They would laugh at the pig eaters loss of business. "Serves them right!" Moreover, the Greeks and Romans frequently used pigs for religious sacrifice, hence a Jew eating pork was considered an apostate and a pagan. Others say that peace of heart given a tortured human being is more important than the loss of a few pigs.

A second question concerns the people's desire to be rid of Jesus as quickly as possible. Strange is it not, since Christ had removed a social menace from their neighborhood and rehabilitated the man who was a former threat to them. You think they would be full of appreciation. Gospel miracles usually excited public acclaim. The Gerasenes are an exception. Perhaps they had a basic hostility to their Jewish neighbors, even an impressive example like Jesus.

Maybe they sympathized with their neighbor who lost his herd and worried that Jesus might affect their own property. Better to urge him to leave. Who could control such a man?

Two Women Cured (Lk. 8:40-56)

Returned to his home country, Jesus was approached by Jairus, the administrator of a synagogue. His daughter was dying. Could Jesus come and heal her? Meanwhile, the crowd crushed against him. In its midst was a woman afflicted with hemorrhages. This blood problem made her ceremonially unclean and caused her shame. Embarrassed to approach Jesus publicly, she secretly touched his garment and hoped for a cure. Jesus stopped and asked who touched him. Peter said that in that shoving and pushing all kinds of people had touched him. Jesus said that someone had touched him in such a way that power flowed from him.

The woman came forward and confessed what she had done and how touching his robe had healed her. Jesus told her that her faith had saved her. She should depart in peace. It was important to emphasize the interpersonal quality of the miracle. Jesus was more than a totem, whose clothes could be touched magically in hopes of a cure. He was a person who came to heal and save people in their freedom. He wanted a personal faith response from them.

It was then that the news arrived that the daughter of Jairus had died. Jesus encouraged Jairus to have faith and his daughter would be saved. Arrived at the house, Jesus met the mourners wailing and crying. He told them to stop the noise for the child was only asleep. They ridiculed him for they knew she was dead. Jesus ignored them, took the parents and Peter, James, and John into the girl's room. He took her by the hand and said, "Child, arise!" The girl arose from the bed and was given into her parents' joyful arms. Jesus added a nice touch by recommending that this young girl needed something to eat.

Reflection

1. If I am listening to a lecture, what happens to me when the speaker tells a story?
2. Why would a purely emotional response to Jesus be "rocky ground" in which roots would not be established?
3. Do I know people caught in the "foot path" of a religion of logic and reason? What is missing in their lives?
4. What examples of people can I cite whose religion is choked by the brambles of a mid-life crisis? How could I respond?
5. Share a "good ground" story of a person whose lovely Christian witness means a great deal to everyone.
6. How could Catholics who hide the lamp of their faith in the privacy of their own minds learn how to share their faith with others?
7. What storms of life have I known where I failed to trust in Christ?
8. What "demons" are there in my life that I need Christ's power to exorcise?
9. How would I help people to treat Jesus as a person and not just a totem as the woman with the hemorrhage was tempted to do?
10. Out of compassion Jesus raised the daughter of Jairus to life. What examples of compassion have I experienced from others?

Prayer

Jesus, Word of love and life, you reach out to me in many different ways. At times I am rocky ground and often I am a thorn bush or a foot path. Enable me to be the good ground that will blossom with love and faith and compassion for others.

9 The Bread and the Cross

A pastor worried about the decline of membership in his parish. He went to see a parishioner who was an insurance executive and asked him the secret of building an expanding clientele. "Ten marbles," replied the executive.

"What do you mean?" asked the pastor.

"When I graduated from college, I went to work for an agency, but did poorly. My territory was filled with young couples who needed insurance protection, but I wasn't reaching them. After a few weeks my boss called me in and told me he was raising my salary. I asked when this would become effective. 'When you become effective,' he said. Then he poured ten red marbles into my hand. He also gave me a card to keep on my desk. The card said, 'Put these ten marbles in your right coat pocket. Now go out and make calls on clients. Each time you complete a call, move one marble from your right pocket to your left one. When all ten marbles are in your left pocket, you are finished for the day. Come back to the office, write up your reports and go home — even if you haven't sold anything.' "

The moral of the story is that the shepherd must go out and look for the sheep. An evangelizing pastor cannot wait for people to come. He must reach out to people in his community and invite them to experience the love and salvation of Jesus and belong to a reconciling, compassionate church community. He must not do this all by himself. He should engage the members of his parish to help by teaching them that by their baptism they are called to build up the Body of Christ.

Jesus Trains His Evangelizers (Lk. 9:1-5)

Jesus did not sit at home in Nazareth waiting for people to come and hear his message and accept him. He traveled from village to village, from town to town, announcing the Good News. He sailed up and down the coast of Galilee preaching, healing, and inviting people to faith and commitment to him and his kingdom.

He also used the "multiplier effect." He could not physically reach everyone, so he trained his disciples to be evangelizers. They were to share their faith in Jesus, his offer of salvation from sin and the kingdom of love, justice, and mercy. They would also conduct a ministry of healing.

Jesus trained them to travel light so that nothing would distract them from their purpose. They were not to take money or food or a suitcase of clothing with them. Instead they should trust in the providence of God and the goodwill offerings of those to whom they ministered. They should not be staying at expensive inns, but ask for hospitality from their listeners. If people rejected them and did not welcome this message, they should move on — shake the dust from their feet — for there were many others hungering for this Gospel and ready to hear and accept it.

The Miracle of the Bread (Lk. 9:10-17)

The preaching of the Word by the apostles is followed by the experience of the miracle of the Bread. Just as in the liturgy, the service of the Word is followed by the service of the sacrament, so in Luke's account the ministry of Word is succeeded by the bread miracle which is a symbol of the sacrament. Having been fed by the words of the Gospel, the people are now fed with the bread of mystery which forecasts the Eucharist.

The apostles had returned from their mission. With Jesus they withdrew in private to Bethsaida. The crowds learned of this and followed them. That evening the apostles told Jesus that he should dismiss the people so they could find a place to eat and lodgings for the night. Jesus said that the apostles should feed them. They protested that all they had was five loaves and two fish. Did Jesus expect them to buy food for all these people? Who had such money?

Jesus instructed them to have the people sit down in groups of fifty. Then in gestures — still used in today's Eucharists — Jesus *took* the *bread*, *looked* up to heaven, spoke a *blessing* and *gave* the food to be distributed. This narrative matches Luke's account of the institution of the Eucharist at the Last supper (22:19) and the scene of the Breaking of the Bread at Emmaus (24:30).

Lose the Self. Take the Cross. Follow Jesus. (Lk. 9:18-27)

Luke connects the first prediction of the passion with this scene of the bread miracle and its eucharistic symbolism. The celebration of the Eucharist is an occasion of table fellowship and the growth of Christian community. But the Eucharist also makes present the saving sacrifice of Jesus on the cross. St. Paul taught this very explicitly. "For as often as you eat this bread and drink this cup, you proclaim the death of the Lord until he comes" (I Cor. 11:26). The Eucharist is therefore a sacrament that both illumines and enables Christian fellowship and mysteriously makes the effective presence and power of the cross available to the participants.

Luke also ties the first prediction of the passion to the confession of Peter and a description of Christian discipleship. Jesus and the apostles had sought solitude for time to pray. In that environment of prayer Jesus asked the apostles who people thought he was. They answered that the crowds varied in their responses, some saying he was John the Baptist, or Elijah or some other prophet come back from the dead. Luke notes that Herod heard the same opinions (9:7-9). Jesus asked the apostles their own judgement. Peter spoke up for them, saying Jesus was "The Messiah of God" (verse 20).

Having made a prediction of his passion, Jesus went on to describe what it meant to be his disciple. Essentially, discipleship contains three elements: (1) Lose your self. (2) Take your cross. (3) Follow Jesus. They would have to follow the same path he walked.

Lose Your Self. This advice seems strange, even forbidding, to a culture that struggles with what is called the "self-worth problem." Again and again therapists point out that low self esteem is at the root of many addictions such as alcoholism and drug abuse, was well as the cycle of child abuse and other intractable personal problems. How can we be called to lose a self that is already shaky and in need of nourishment and affirmation?

Jesus would be just as compassionate and sensitive as we are to the self-worth difficulties. He said himself that the healthy do not need a doctor. The sick do. His healing ministry addressed that need. How often he said after a miracle that the person cured had been made "whole." Once wholeness had been achieved, then the person could be invited to discipleship. Today, Jesus would say that the first step is to make a person whole by creating a strong valuing of the self, using both therapeutic and spiritual means, the latter helping a person appreciate having a self made in God's image of love and beauty. The person whose self esteem is restored is ready for the path of discipleship.

A second problem raised by Christ's call to lose the self is the negative way of denial of self that seems morbid to many people. This bruises the modern sensibility. Examples of asceticism drawn from the lives of Christian disciples in other ages of church history repel rather than attract today's believers. Such spiritual lifestyles do not appeal even to the most idealistic of today's Christians.

The problem with that model is that, rightly or wrongly, it seems too negative. Is there not a positive method for following Christ's call? Is it possible any longer? Yes, when the path of discipleship is seen as self-transcendence. This means letting go of that side of the self that draws us away from love. With God's help we must transcend the aspects of self that impede the growth of love and the liberating impact of God's grace. In this pursuit we may not be adopting the punishing asceticisms of the past, but we will still have a difficult, challenging, demanding lifestyle. That is why Jesus spoke of the cross.

Take Your Cross. Jesus invites us to take the hero journey to the cross and resurrection. Nothing worthwhile is ever achieved easily. As the T-shirts on ski slopes say, "No guts — No glory." It is not easy to let go of sin or selfishness. The asceticism of letting go is one of the most difficult challenges that face us. My nature fears conversion and change. I am afraid I will be changed to someone who is not me. I must become convinced that love will change me into who I really am.

The cross asks us to leave self behind so that we can live lives of self-less relationships and self-less responsibility. Our concentration shifts from the self to the other, and ultimately to the greatest of all others, Jesus Christ. At first this feels like it is too much to give up. We hate it. We fear it. But when we transcend our fear and hate, we discover the real selves God has buried deep within us.

These are the selves of power, the selves of love, the selves of responsibility. Living in contact with original love — that from God — makes us feel we are experiencing a perpetual Easter. Our superficial selves felt inadequate, ever battling the forces of distraction and destruction. When we transcend them, we sink deep inside to the still point, the place of the real self that draws powerful love from God. We are at the fountain of the greatest creativity and the deepest concentration. Then we praise God for the gift of the glorious cross that made this possible.

Follow Me. The third step of discipleship is following Christ. We have already done this by transcending our selves and taking up the cross. Following Jesus means leaning upon him alone. We come to the point where we trust absolutely in him and surrender to his plans for us. We let go our of own plans for holiness and listen for Christ's guidance. Even when we feel a sense of a loss of direction, we rest in Christ without fail.

We avoid trying to control Christ's actions and give up the desire to know exactly where we are on the faith journey. We ask to be an ideal disciple, but we leave it to Jesus to determine what kind of disciple that will be. We surrender to Jesus because Jesus has surrendered himself to us. Jesus loved us without reserve. We reply with as much love as we can in a similar manner. We let go of our selves so that Jesus can live for us. We stop possessing even our souls, for Christ's love possesses them instead.

The Transfiguration — Glory on a Mountain (Lk. 9:28-36)

One of the persistent problems of the Christian religion is that its members spend too much time with religious words and thoughts that are not based on an experience of Jesus. Many people study theology but never experience the love that flows from direct contact with Jesus. They substitute word games and scholar's one-upmanship for the joyful exchange of affection between themselves and Christ. The "blah-blah" of the din of religious words replaces the exultation of a direct encounter with the divine.

Theology is obviously supremely important, but it works best when it shimmers with the vitality of a spirituality that grounds it. Real religious discourse should be like God talking through the lips of people who devote time each day to meditative prayer. It should be more than brain-to-brain exchange or a dull transfer of abstractions from one little gray cell to another. Position papers divorced from religious experience are tiresome. One has the right to hear the echo of love in the religious words that are spoken.

This is the principal message of the Transfiguration of Jesus. Peter, James and John — the select three whom Jesus singled out for special training — have heard many of Christ's sermons. His words have flooded their ears and perhaps begun to cling to their brains. They had experienced Jesus as a person, felt his affection for them, sensed the power of his personality, and witnessed his remarkable miraculous powers.

What they needed was a defining experience to gather the diverse strands of Christ's impact on them into a more unified force. Jesus wanted to reach them at the most silent part of their souls when they would feel love as never before. He wanted to enlighten them in a far deeper manner than he had up to this time. He took them up to a mountain to pray. He often drew them to meditation. They were now ready for one of the more profound effects of meditative prayer. They sank into a tranquility in which they were asleep to the world around them but wide awake to the spiritual presence of Jesus.

They beheld Christ's glory. Light caused his face to shine like the sun and his clothes to become white as snow. They were doing more than merely physically looking "at" Jesus. (One can see the sun, but when its warmth is felt then it opens one up with its pleasant embrace.) Their intimacy with Jesus transformed them. The transfiguration of Jesus was a transformation of the apostles.

Jesus enlightened them, meaning that his light entered into their inmost being. This religious experience put meaning into the words and deeds they had heard and seen. Up to this time they believed that what Jesus said was true. Now it "seemed" true as well. They knew it with more than their brains. They accepted him with their hearts.

In that mystical enlightenment event, they saw Moses and Elijah talking with Jesus. They heard of Christ's exodus — his forthcoming saving death and resurrection. Peter wanted this moment to last forever. He wanted to contain love in physical shrines for Jesus, Moses, and Elijah. He did not know what he was saying, for such a unique and transcendent experience is too personal to be fully expressed in a physical representation.

As the enlightenment event came to a close, a shining cloud enveloped them, a cloud of "unknowing" in the human sense. It is a paradox, a seeming contradiction, for the cloud stills the reason and yet fills the whole person with light. They hear God the Father affirm that Jesus is his Son to whom they should listen.

This was a lot to take in all at once. "They fell silent" (verse 36). A religious experience of this magnitude can only be assimilated in the quiet of one's being. The mystery would silently unfold in each one of them until they had the images and words that would give the world some inkling of that astonishing event on the mountain.

Jesus Resolves to Go to Jerusalem (Lk. 9:43-62)

Luke relentlessly keeps the theme of the cross alive throughout all of this. The first prediction of the passion followed the bread miracle. Now a second prediction of the passion follows the ecstasy of the Transfiguration. Even in the midst of that event, Jesus conversed with Moses and Elijah about his "exodus," the Christian passover that would accomplish our salvation.

Jesus knew he had to prepare his apostles for the mystery of his death and resurrection. He was more than a popular preacher who happened to be involved in some unfortunate controversies with religious leaders. It was only natural that they thought he would work things out. Eventually, people would come to see things his way. His eloquence and obvious compassion would win everybody over. Jesus warned them that dark days lay ahead. The gospel says they did not understand him, meaning they refused to accept what he was saying. Most people use psychological denial to block out what is too unpleasant to contemplate. They were no exceptions to this rule.

Secretly, they believed he was really a political messiah who would somehow establish a religious kingdom on earth where God's rule was embodied in a government system with themselves as the "power partners and rulers." In fact Jesus heard them arguing about who might be the top people in that government.

So he took a little child and placed that child before them. Children do not rule nations. Child princes have adult regents to do that for them. Jesus knew that they loved children and received them as sources of affection and love. He told them that in the future kingdom that is how he was to be welcomed and received, not as an emperor full of force and power, but a child full of simplicity and love. Not the love of power, but the power of love would be the ruling policy of the kingdom.

The message was hard to put across as became immediately evident when they passed through Samaritan territory among people traditionally hostile to them. True to form, the Samaritans refused them hospitality. So angry were the apostles that they asked Jesus if they could curse the people with fire from heaven to burn them up. They still lived by the principle of "love of power." Jesus sighed and rebuked them for their unworthy sentiments.

At various places Jesus invited people to follow him. One man said that he must first bury his father. Jesus told him to let the dead bury the dead. Another said he must say farewell to his family. Jesus replied that once the hand is on the plow a person should never look back. This does not mean that Jesus was insensitive to a mourning son or to the responsibility to one's family. He was using the occasion as a metaphor for understanding how absolute a commitment he eventually wanted from those who would be his disciples.

From now on in Luke, Christ's eyes are fixed on the cross and the resurrection. "When the days for his being taken up were fulfilled, he resolutely determined to journey to Jerusalem" (verse 51).

Reflection

1. How would I apply to myself the story of the "Ten Marbles" cited at the beginning of this chapter?
2. Jesus trained his evangelizers to travel light — no money, no change of clothes. How would I translate that advice for my evangelizing work today?

3. What is the connection between the bread miracle and the first prediction of the passion?
4. What details of the bread miracle remind me of the Eucharist?
5. How is the Eucharist a sacrament both of fellowship and the power of the cross?
6. In what ways do I practice losing my "self" in order to be Christ's disciple?
7. What does taking my cross mean for me?
8. Why does following Christ mean that I let him determine where I am on the road of love and holiness?
9. What aspects of the Transfiguration seem like a deep meditation?
10. Why is meditation necessary for putting some life into the religious words and concepts I use?

Prayer

Dear Christ of glory, you enlightened Peter, James, and John in your Transfiguration. The experience transformed them. In the cloud of "unknowing," they received insight into the mystery of your love. Bring me to that kind of intimacy that draws me out of my darkness into your enabling light.

10   How to Be a Catholic Evangelizer

G.K. Chesterton met one evening with a few of his literary friends. In the middle of their stimulating conversation, one of them posed this question: "If you were isolated on a desert island and could have only one book, which one would you choose?"

One person said, "I would choose the Bible."

Another ventured, "The works of William Shakespeare."

When Chesterton's turn came, he impishly stated, "I would pick *Thomas' Guide to Practical Shipbuilding*."

Christ's Practical Guide to Evangelizing (Lk. 10:1-24)

At the beginning of chapter 9, Luke outlined briefly Christ's training of the apostles for their evangelizing ministry. Luke begins this chapter with a fuller description of Christ's practical guidelines for evangelizing. Jesus has appointed seventy-two other missionaries. The "multiplier effect" advances with the addition of these new evangelizers. Even these will not be enough. Jesus told them the harvest is enormous compared to the small number of evangelizers. His first guideline dwelt on the need to "pray" for more workers.

Wisely, Jesus sent them out in pairs, as a small support group, so that one can encourage and inspire the other. He left them under no illusion that this would be easy. He cautioned them to think of themselves as lambs among wolves. Again he reiterated his policy of traveling light. If they own little they will have less to think about. The more you possess the more the possessions preoccupy you. The more you own the less you give. The less you have the more you give. Poverty generates freedom which is at the heart of the Gospel they will proclaim. Material things are not the only source of joy. Something is greater than that, the peace in one's heart resulting from love and reconciliation with self, others, and God.

Jesus counseled them to enter a home with the word of peace on their lips. A peaceful host will accept this greeting. If the person has shut peace out then the peace greeting will return to the evangelists. Behind this mysterious saying is the Hebrew concept of the power of speech. In an oral culture, speech was more than mere communication. The spoken word was thought to have power to produce what was said, especially in the case of blessings and curses.

In our document culture, where the written word has legal force, it is the written contract or will that has binding force. If it is written it must be true. Lawyers spend a lot of time following a paper trail in preparing a legal brief. But in the oral culture of Bible times, Christ's counsel about giving peace to another by means of the word of peace was thought to have effective power if the recipient was open to the peace that was offered. The spoken word seemed to have an almost physical dynamism. If the peace word was not accepted, it would return to the giver.

Jesus gave them prudent advice about staying in one home in the town or village they visited. The process of evangelizing should be balanced by the stability symbolized by staying in one base of operations. Their energies should be saved for the mission and not diluted by constant distracting moves. Moreover, they should have the good humor and delicacy to eat what was set before them and not be fussy about the cuisine. They should concentrate on their mission alone and not let unpalatable food choices get in the way (let alone offend their hosts).

Jesus reminded them that the Gospel is offered in freedom to each human being. They should present it with love and illustrate its inherent attractiveness. But people are free to accept or reject it. There was no point in trying to force it down the throats of their listeners. If the people are closed to the message, then the evangelists should conserve their energies, shake the dust from their feet, and move on to more promising converts. The harvest potential was tremendous. The evangelizers should move on to the great number of those waiting to hear and accept the Good News of salvation from sin and Christ's kingdom of love, justice, and mercy.

Christ's commission to evangelize continues in today's church. His advice to the seventy-two disciples remains relevant for evangelizers in our own day. An effective evangelization plan would include the following adaptations of Christ's counsel.

(1) *Witness Jesus.* Jesus personally witnessed his message by his loving and compassionate presence, his preaching of the Good News, and his invitation to people to accept him, his message and his church. Modern people listen more readily to witnesses. If they listen to the teachers, it is because the teachers witness what they say. The positive witness of a loving, caring and concerned Catholic is the strongest method of attracting people to Jesus and the church. No one should feel like a stranger in our midst. We should be a welcoming church.

The parish will attract new members when it is a welcoming community. One Catholic who had lived in eight different cities said that he had never encountered a real welcome into a parish community. He found one church where the liturgy was fairly good, but the people had to be coaxed into singing and participating. There was no social interaction with other parishioners. On the other hand a great number of parishes are welcoming and celebrating communities. Uncaring communities will not be magnets for Christ. Loving ones will grow.

(2) *Share Your Faith.* The second step in evangelizing is to share your faith and to explain the teachings of Christ in terms of what it means to be a Catholic. Silent witness is not enough. No matter how excellent a witness is, there is still the need to say what it means. It requires an unambiguous sharing of the teachings of Christ. Jesus was the greatest witness who ever lived, yet he ceaselessly explained what his witness meant for daily life.

Jesus' Sermon on the Mount, his parables and dialogues with people show us how to share our faith with others. These meditations on the gospels are designed to help with such sharing of faith. The more we are devoted to meditative praying and studying of the Bible, the more we will be effective evangelizers — witnessing and sharing our faith in Christ.

(3) *Make This a Person-to-Person Ministry.* People attract people. Love begets love. There are 17,000,000 inactive Catholics in the United States. One-third of them would most likely return to the Church if they received a warm invitation to come home again. Redemptorist Father William McKee dramatizes this with the following conversation.

"Hey Father, I used to be a Catholic."

"How long ago?"

"Well, over twenty years."

"Have you ever thought of coming back?"

"Many times."

"Why didn't you?"

"Because nobody asked me."

We need not be shy about a friendly invitation to return home to our parish.

(4) *Challenge the Culture.* Jesus challenged the hypocrisy of those who would stone the adulterous woman. He spoke out against the powerful who imposed heavy burdens on the poor. He criticized religious leaders who reduced the faith to little practices and neglected the more important aspects of religion, such as mercy and fidelity. Jesus asks us to speak up on behalf of the poor and homeless and to strengthen the institutions of marriage and the family and to raise our children with respect for the virtues of peace and justice. We should not segregate our religious life from life in our culture. The Gospel has the power to purify culture. When outsiders see this, they will be drawn to investigate a church that has such a positive impact on society.

(5) *Support the Good Efforts of the Culture.* Advances in medicine should be used in the service of life. The media could be a strong force for strengthening family values. High-Tech should be employed in the improvement of human life. The Gospel can regenerate the good developments in our culture and make sure they support a decent life for all people. Our church did this before for a pagan Roman Empire, barbarian hordes, and the unbelievers of the Enlightenment. We can be a creative spiritual force in today's technology. High-Tech needs the High-Touch of the spiritual and moral power of the Gospel. The technical human is still the same old human hungering for love, affection, and salvation. A church that offers this response will attract new members.

When the seventy-two evangelizers returned with the reports of their successes and failures, they mentioned that they had very little acceptance from Chorazin and Bethsaida and even Capernaum. These were all well known religious towns, proud of their religious observance. However, they refused to accept a message that implied they should probe deeper and look at their inner moral and spiritual attitudes. They kept the rules. Was not that enough? Jesus assailed the spiritual pride of these cities and said that pagan cities like Tyre and Sidon would have repented and believed long ago if such deeds and words had been heard in their communities. Like the menacing prophets of old, Jesus uttered harsh words for these stubborn people, "You shall be thrown down to hell" (verse 15, *Jerusalem Bible*).

At the same time the evangelizers were ecstatic about their successes. They seemed very impressed at their ability to drive out demons. Jesus told them he saw Satan fall like lightning from the sky. He reminded them that he had given them the power over the demons as symbolized in poisonous serpents and scorpions. Still, they should not be too impressed with this. Far greater is the assurance that their names — that is, their lives — are inscribed in heaven.

Jesus personalized their evangelizing work. To listen to them was to listen to him. To reject them was to reject him. Hence a real evangelizer is one who faithfully witnesses Christ and his message. Their excitement moved Jesus to sing a hymn of praise to the Father for the good work of these evangelizers. They had learned his teaching about being childlike and so touched many hearts, rather than relying on being wise and learned, appealing just to the brain without reaching the heart. In an aside Jesus privately told them how fortunate they were to be part of this evangelizing ministry. Prophets and kings had hoped to be part of this development but never lived to see it. "Blessed are the eyes that see what you see" (verse 23).

The Supremacy of Love
and the Good Samaritan (Lk. 10:25-37)

In an animated discussion a scholar of the Torah asked Jesus what one must do to inherit this mysterious eternal life he was offering to Jew and non-Jew alike. Jesus asked him what the Bible said about ideal Jewish behavior. The scholar replied by quoting Leviticus 19:18 about loving God with all one's heart and Deuteronomy 6:5 concerning loving the neighbor as oneself. Jesus approved his reply and called the scholar to practice what he just quoted and he would receive eternal life just like anyone else.

The scholar, however, was not satisfied because the term neighbor in the second quote usually only applied to the members of the Jewish covenant people. That is why he asked Jesus to clarify what he meant by neighbor. Jesus replied with the famous parable of the Good Samaritan. The following background can help appreciate the parable.

It is twenty-three miles from Jericho to Jerusalem. The road twists and turns between steep and barren cliffs that are nearly 4,000 feet high. What dangerous inner city streets are to contemporary Americans, the Jericho-Jerusalem road was to citizens of New Testament Palestine. Surviving police records tell of numerous assaults along this road. St. Jerome reported that even in the fourth century it was called the "bloody road."

Jesus used this well known and fearful route as the setting for an awareness session on the meaning of neighbor. He described a vicious robbery and the reaction of three people to the victim. By noting that the victim traveled alone, he reduced sympathy for him. He should have known better and journeyed with a group for mutual protection.

First came the priest who saw the victim and passed on. One would expect the priest as an religious leader committed to model biblical values to stop and help the victim. Priests preached love of neighbor. They should practice their words by lending a helping hand. This priest may have been afraid of touching what looked like a dead body. If he touched the body he would be ritually unclean for seven days and thus deprived of temple service — and salary. It would be too much trouble to get involved. Besides, he might have been low on cash.

Next came the Levite, the equivalent of a modern deacon. As a public religious figure, he also should show loving care for one in need. The law permitted him to touch dead bodies. Perhaps he feared this was a decoy, like a modern driver alone on an interstate highway seeing a body on the road. The Levite knew tales of people stopping to help a person only to be assaulted by robbers suddenly appearing and brutalizing the charitable one. He preferred his own safety to caring for the victim.

Last came the Samaritan an object of scorn and bigotry to the Jews hearing the story. This would be like introducing a black hero to a group of racists or a female heroine to a band of sexists. Jews repudiated Samaritans on religious and political grounds. The history of their mutual hatred was a long and painful one.

The lawyer asked Jesus to define a neighbor as though certain people because of their religion and ethnic origin could not be one. Jesus shifted the argument to neighborliness. Jesus changed the perspective from the person to be helped to the helping one. It is not a question of deciding who is worthy of my assistance, but of an attitude which says all human beings are deserving of my care and affection.

The fear of strangers is a common enough attitude. It is rationalized by using stereotypes to justify non-involvement with those who are presumably not worthy of our attention. This is systematic hatred and organized fear. Ingrained in religious people, such an attitude is especially regrettable and vicious. Jesus taught that the real neighbor is not the one to be loved but the one that does the loving of any other person regardless of race, creed, color, sex, age or any other reason. When risk is involved the test is greater. The Samaritan proved to be a neighbor. That is the lesson for all Christians.

Martha's Busy-ness and Mary's Attentiveness (Lk. 10:38-42)

A contemplative nun tells the story of people's reaction to her choice to enter a cloister. "My parents felt I was burying myself. But in the same breath they were good enough to say, 'You're at peace. We understand. We think you're crazy, but if this will make you happy, then we'll be happy.' My friends asked questions such as, 'Why don't you give to God by giving to people directly?' "

The members of her order meditate for two hours every day and chant the full Liturgy of the Hours. They take care of household tasks and the gardening. They make communion breads for a source of income. They may visit with their families on Christmas, Easter and their birthdays. They have two community recreation periods a day. There is no TV except for some special religious programming. Silence and prayer and contemplation constitute their ministry.

Sister commented on her prayer experience. "The longer I am here, the more my heart becomes sensitive to God. When I am with God it is not important to have words or images. God knows my inner needs. A poet has said that in love one may experience the pain of too much tenderness. I find that in the contemplative life, more than in any other way, I experience Christ's love and goodness — even his pain."

The nun had been an active Martha for many years before entering the cloister. She knew what it was like to be a salesperson in a department store, a secretary to the vice-president of a large hospital, and a worker in the circulation section of a big city newspaper. She did not dislike her activist years. She just felt the call to the silent life of meditation and prayer.

The Martha-Mary story has something to do with one's natural inclination. Some people are born activists. Others prefer peace and quiet. Some are aggressive accomplishers. Others do not mind a little dreaming. Some are as busy as bees. Others are like the lazing coals in a fireplace.

Quiet personalities make good researchers and contemplatives. If they happen to be called to the contemplative life, they follow a natural bent. It is a case of grace building on nature. However, this is not true in every case. Some of the church's greatest contemplatives, such as Teresa of Avila and Bernard of Clairvaux, were hyper-active personalities, even by our standards.

Some activists have little sympathy for the people who enjoy silence and thinking. Those who just sit there do not seem to be contributing anything to society. That is the value judgement of certain activists. In fact, high moments of creative genius occur, more often than not, in quiet and withdrawn environments. Society and religion need both the activists and the quiet ones.

When Jesus entered the home of Martha and Mary, he was feeling a heavy burden in his heart, for he was coping with his decision to face a dangerous situation in Jerusalem. He might die for what he stood for in the very near future. His internal seriousness needed some quiet and silent healing. The last thing he needed was a lot of fussing over him. He sought the company of someone who would simply "let him be."

His experience reminds us of the need to be sensitive to the needs of people at given times in their lives. Jesus needed quiet. There will be other times for partying and activity.

So it is in the church. Some will follow the call to the cloister and the life of prayer. Others pursue active ministries. Both ministries offer their healing to those in need of one or the other. Activists need a time of prayer each day. Contemplatives have their own work responsibilities every day. They pray for the rest of us. At the same time all of us should have time for prayer so that our actions may proceed from love and faith. We honor both Martha and Mary as saints. We thank Jesus for their gifts.

Reflection

1. When I hear the word evangelization what kind of effect does it have upon me?
2. In oral cultures the word of peace was effective when it was received by the listeners. What are examples today of words that have an effect on listeners?
3. What are some examples I can cite which illustrate how a person-to-person approach has drawn someone into the church?
4. What are some issues in the culture that my faith motivates me to criticize?
5. What are some elements in our society that deserve my faith approval and support?
6. Jesus personalized the evangelizing process by saying that listening to his evangelizers means listening to him. What would that mean for my evangelizing ministry?
7. What are some modern Good Samaritan stories I can share?
8. Where do I find my Christian call to be a neighbor to everyone is challenged?
9. As I look at my own personality, am I inclined to be an activist or a quiet one?
10. Why does the church need contemplatives?

Prayer

Jesus, you commissioned me and all the baptized to share our faith in you with others. Even though I know a person-to-person ministry is effective, I still feel shy about it. Grant me the courage and motivation I need to invite people to experience your love and forgiveness and membership in a reconciling community.

11 The Art and Practice of Prayer

Humor is the beginning of faith and laughter is the beginning of prayer.

—Reinhold Niebuhr

More things are wrought by prayer
Than this world dreams of.
Wherefore, let thy voice
Rise like a fountain for me day and night.

—Alfred, Lord Tennyson

An old woman tells a story of how she was in a hospital and full of pain. She did not have the courage to take the tests that would tell her what was wrong. One morning a member of her church visited her and told her that a group of her friends was forming a prayer circle for her. They were planning to spend a whole night to pray for her. That night she slept like a child and in the morning was strong enough to take the needed tests.

Dr. Alexis Carrel writes, "Make a habit of sincere prayer. Then your life will be noticeably changed. Prayer is the world's most powerful form of energy."

PBS TV's Bill Moyers has produced a memorable program on what he says is America's most popular sung prayer, the hymn "Amazing Grace." Written by John Newton, an English sea captain who had once been in the slave trade, the prayer reflected his conversion from his immoral business because of the power of God's grace.

Lord, Teach Us To Pray (Lk. 11:1-13)

Luke's gospel is a gospel of prayer. Luke shows us Jesus at prayer before the great events of his life. Jesus prayed at his baptism and before his first conflict with the Pharisees and his choice of the twelve apostles. In Luke we see Jesus praying just before he asks the disciples who he is and prior to his first prediction of the passion. Jesus prays at the Transfiguration, on the cross, and he promises to pray for Peter when Peter faced the hour of his great temptation. Only in Luke are the prayer parables of the friend at midnight and the unjust judge. Luke remembers for us the fact that Jesus did more than invite us to pray. Jesus witnessed prayer over and over again at significant stages in his ministry and regularly in deep meditation.

Christ's disciples had ample opportunity to observe Jesus at prayer. He prayed often and for long periods of time. The gospels generally say little about what his prayer was like. Was he reciting or singing psalms? Was he whispering a series of short prayers as in a mantra? Was he absorbed in the long deep silences of meditation?

We do have some clues. St. John's gospel records Christ's Last Supper discourse in which he publicly speaks to his Father with warmth and intimacy. In this eleventh chapter of Luke we hear Jesus teaching us to pray the Our Father. One thing is clear, the apostles were so moved by the beauty and obvious depth of Christ's prayer that they asked him how to do it themselves.

Jesus responded by teaching them the Our Father. This was not simply another prayer formula. It was a lesson in the attitudes that should accompany our praying. The Our Father deserves some extensive commentary, but a few preliminary thoughts should precede this reflection.

Our lead comes from St. Augustine's letter on prayer, addressed to a prominent woman of his times, the Lady Proba. Augustine's basic message is that prayer is the expression of our inborn desire to be happy. The quest for happiness is the greatest motivator in the world. The thirst for happiness moves some people to seek it by getting rich, acquiring power, or participating in unlimited sexual pleasure. Money, power, and sex have mobilized the energies of millions of people because they believe these goals are the secret of happiness.

At first these methods seem to work and some happiness is obtained. Yet, after every million earned, every power position plundered, and every sexual object attained, there follows a sadness and futile emptiness. These goals supply only a temporary joy, not enduring happiness. Worse yet, the more money, sex, and power one obtains, the less payoff there is in real satisfaction.

It is all an illusion. It always was. It always will be. These well known facts of life teach us two lessons. First, our undying need to be happy makes many of us look for it in the wrong places, such as in money, power, and sex. Secondly, this type of quest never works.

Jesus was the happiest human being who ever lived, despite setback, disappointments, and sufferings. He never sought happiness in wealth, position, and sexuality. He had no money to pay for a house. He rejected power when people wanted to make him a king. He chose a celibate lifestyle. Jesus was not opposed to people having enough money for a decent way of life, or reasonable control over one's life situation, or a sexuality in marriage that reflected the lifelong love of the spouses. He did not stand against the proper use of these things, so much as their abuse.

He showed us, however, that he was happy because he equated his personal desire for joy with his desire for God. It is the same reality. God *is* happiness. God is the source of all true and lasting joy. Each act of getting closer to God is progress in personal happiness. Money, power, and sex are happiness substitutes. God is the real producer of contentment. The day we see our desire for absolute satisfaction is truly our desire for God, then we will be on the authentic path to bliss. Then we will realize why prayer is important. Then we will unlock the mystery and meaning of the Our Father.

Prayer time is time devoted to nourishing our desire for unlimited happiness, because it intensifies our desire to be nearer to God. Prayer is meant to enlarge our capacity for happiness. It opens our hearts wider to receive God. After all, it was the Lord who invented happiness and created us to enjoy life with God on earth and in eternal life hereafter.

No eye can see this, for it has no color. No ear can hear it, for it has no sound. Happiness is a spiritual gift that comes from a spiritual source. Prayer is an exercise of our inborn desire to be happy. The more we exercise that desire, the more we can receive this gift that God very much wants to give us. Such happiness does not come easily.

Praying is hard work. Praying leads us to lose the self and take the cross and follow Jesus. Prayer moves us to search for happiness in these acts that at first glance would seem to make us unhappy. Yet all people, whose faith, hope, and love moves them to try this despite all appearances, tell us that it works. We must use spiritual means to get what is essentially a spiritual gift. All other efforts are illusory and will fail.

Jesus knows we are not angels. Each day we will need prayer words to remind ourselves of our desire for happiness and the way to achieve it. This is the purpose of prayer words and formulas. This is why David wrote the Psalms, the greatest collection of prayer words ever composed. This is why Jesus gave us the Our Father, the greatest single prayer in the world.

Besides vocal prayer, we also need time each day for silent meditation. The stress of modern life will cool our conscious desire for God. Specified times for daily prayer stir up our desire for God and increase our yearning for enduring contentment. Lots of words are not necessary. Plenty of fervent desire is. Augustine tells us that more is accomplished through sighs than speech, more is achieved with tears than words. Such prayer creates the most pleasant of all discoveries — that we can find the secret of happiness.

The above reflection is the necessary background for under-standing Christ's teachings on prayer in the eleventh chapter of Luke. Our desire for happiness is the pre-condition for appreciating the petitions of the Our Father.

Our Father, who art in heaven. Jesus begins his teaching on prayer by turning us immediately to the presence of God and his dwelling place — the fountain of all happiness. "My soul longs for you, O God. Athirst is my soul for God. I had rather one day in your courts than a thousand elsewhere" (Ps. 42:2; 84:10). The proper search for joy begins with attention on its origin in God. This is a goal statement.

If we will to reach this goal, we shall will the means to achieve it. Clarity of purpose must precede the choice of methods. Spiritual power is directly related to the grand passion to reach the goal that is never forgotten. Many people spend too much time on methods and techniques of praying. They become so absorbed in the means that they waste their energies on the process and forget the purpose of the process. Jesus tells us to keep our eyes on the prize — absolute joy in union with God.

Hallowed be thy name. Jesus says the second step in prayer is an act of praise and gratitude to God for the gift of joy. This act of praise surges from us spontaneously in the midst of our exaltation. Immediate and personal experience of God fills us with the assurance of divine trustworthiness so gracious and sensitive. Feeling this in the radiance of God's love releases our natural urge to praise. This form of prayer arises less from logic than from experience. When we are in love with God, the push to praise the Lord will come unbidden to our lips. We praise God before we petition anything for ourselves or others. Praise precedes any other form of petition in Christ's prayer priorities. "Praise the Lord, O my soul. I will praise the Lord as long as I live" (Ps. 146:1-2).

Thy will be done. God is love. This means that God wills only our happiness and personal fulfillment. A real lover can only will good — never evil — to the beloved. The evils and sufferings that befall us result from our personal sins and the sins of society. Good and bad people alike suffer the inevitable adversities of life. The love of God does not protect us from the pain of living. God's love, however, fills us with the power to cope with and overcome the trials of life. God's armor of affection enables us to stand our ground when things are at their worst.

Jesus did not promise us a rose garden, a life without sorrow. His best advice to us asks us to "Lose the self. . . . Take the Cross. . . . Follow him." Not pain avoidance, but confrontation with it is Christ's formula for happiness. This does not mean we should look for trouble, but resolutely accept it in union with Christ when it comes. The experience that promises to hurt at first turns out to be a healing event.

This will only make sense to those who have lost self and identify with God's will instead. As long as our own will dominates, we shall never understand the cross. Only when we surrender our will (not easy by any means, not even for Christ as the Gethsemane scene illustrates), and let God's will take over, will the cross make sense. So long as our will is in charge, we will never be truly happy. True joy occurs in the lives of those who practice "Thy will be done."

Give us this day our daily bread. The mechanics for human survival — delivery of goods and services, money to buy them, jobs to get the money — bond our attention and energies so strongly that we rarely think of God as the absolute source of our survival and development. Saints of every age, including our own time, tell us that trust in God for our daily needs does work. Christ simply asks us to get beyond the mechanics of living and focus on the wonder of life's ultimate source — God, from whom all blessings flow. That is why Jesus performed the bread miracles and gave us the Eucharist which embodies what all survival and development truly means. The Lord will be able to give us the daily bread of happiness when we depend on God to do it.

Forgive us our trespasses as we forgive those who trespass against us. Each time we enact this most divine form of love, we will experience forgiveness. Every time I forgive someone, I am receiving graces of forgiveness. Mercy begets mercy. The forgiving person is the forgiven person. The reconciler is the reconciled. Christ has given us the Sacrament of Reconciliation where we experience peace with God, neighbor, and self. The sacrament celebrates our commendable acts of forgiveness as well as granting us God's formal forgiveness of our own sins. This sacrament reinforces our habit of mercy. The sacrament expands our grateful awareness that Christ's redemptive power makes possible the habit of mercy that makes our lives worth living. The more forgiving we become, the easier it is to be forgiven.

Lead us not into temptation, but deliver us from evil. There will never be a life without temptation, test, and trial. Jesus does not advise us to pray for a trouble-free life. That would be unrealistic. Jesus urges us to pray to overcome the temptations we will encounter. With God's grace, we can conquer temptations to sin. Moreover, God will not let us be tested beyond our ability to endure. "God is faithful and will not let you be tried beyond your strength; but with the trial he will also provide a way out, so that you may be able to bear it" (I Cor. 10:13). Perfect happiness only happens in heaven. On earth there will be trials and evils. Our happiness here is imperfect. Jesus ends the Our Father on this note of realism, but always with a tone of hope, for we have help in temptation and the promise of deliverance from evils. Jesus is a loving savior and we are the beloved.

Jesus concluded his teaching on prayer with an example of perseverance in prayer (the persistent friend) and an example of God's understanding of our needs (the loving parent).

The Real Value of a Supernatural Sign (Lk. 11:14-36)

Christ performed an exorcism which led his enemies to say he did it by the power of the devil. Jesus exposed their lack of logic by saying the devil is not likely to send a demon to expel a demon. His miracles are faith events, belief being required to experience a miracle and faith demanded for recognizing the miracle as an act of God. Christ's critics, lacking faith, do not perceive the supernatural reality of his signs.

Jesus Condemns Hypocrites and Legalists (Lk. 11:37-54)

Hypocrisy and legalism have always given religion a bad name. Satires about churches have a never failing source of material in the lives of pompous clerics and pretentious laity. No modern critic of religion could out-perform Christ's criticism of the hypocrisy and legalism of some of the religious leaders of his time. Luke assembles Christ's various "Woe Statements" here at the end of chapter eleven. His thunderous and unambiguous condemnations speak for themselves.

Religious hypocrites still ruin our modern times. Religious legalists still exist to make us do what they would not do. It may sober us to know that sometimes we also sin in this way. Let us humbly pray for deliverance from this evil in others and ourselves.

Reflection

1. How can I tell that I have an inborn desire to be happy?
2. In what sense can I say that my desire for happiness is identical to my desire for God?
3. How does the theme of my desire for happiness relate to these words: "Our Father, who art in heaven"?

4. How can I understand that the act of prayer is the exercise of my yearning for joy?
5. Why is the prayer of praise so natural and spontaneous in my quest for happiness?
6. Why does my preoccupation with the mechanics of survival need the balancing of the "Give us this day our daily bread"?
7. What do I mean when I pray, "Lead us not into temptation?"
8. If Christ wills only our happiness, what am I to think of all the evils I cause and put up with in this world?
9. Why do we still have religious hypocrites despite all the criticism leveled at them?
10. What are some stories of religious legalism that bother me?

Prayer

Jesus, teach me to pray just as you did when the apostles asked you for such training. Strengthen my life with the attitudes of the Our Father. Lead me to see that my desire for happiness comes from you and that you are indeed the one who can fulfill that desire.

12 Insecurity of Fear —
Security of Faith

Two Kinds of Preachers — Prophets and Wisdom Speakers

The Hebrew covenant contains two kinds of preaching: prophetic utterance and wisdom speaking. Prophets like Isaiah and Jeremiah preached fiery sermons about the sins of injustice and infidelity to the covenant. They urged their listeners to undergo moral and spiritual conversion. The prophets gave emotional talks filled with vivid images and urgent passion.

Wisdom speakers such as Sirach and Solomon preached quite differently. Generally, they did not address the burning social issues of their times. While the books of the prophets have the tart flavor of headline news, the wisdom books sound calmer, less topical, more like homespun philosophy.

The wisdom sayers love to compose memorable proverbs, axioms, and helpful hints for daily life. If the prophets communicate a fiery sense of immediacy, the wise ones impart the long range view of life. Theirs is the world of universal truths, common sense advice, and conclusions arising from hard won human experience. They are the kind of people who would say: "Good judgment is the product of experience. But experience is the product of bad judgments."

They say little about the affairs of state, but a good deal about the affairs of the heart. We have seen and will see that Jesus was quite capable of preaching prophetically. At times he also acted the prophet, especially in his cleansing of the temple. However, a significant portion of his preaching sounded more like the wise one talking in the tradition of the wisdom speakers.

Such is the case of Christ's preaching recorded in the twelfth chapter of Luke which is presently before us. Luke has collected these sayings from various sources. The material which at first seems so diverse and disconnected can be sorted out into three topics: Stop worrying. Prepare for death. Be countercultural.

Stop Worrying (Lk. 12:1-34)

Jesus begins his wisdom talk by persuading us to stop worrying and start living a life of faith. The security of faith should replace the insecurity of worry based on material concerns. He takes another jab at the hypocrisy of the Pharisees so that he can ask us, by contrast, to live open, real, and sincere lives. That should be our goal. The demon of fear can cause an obsession with material needs to the neglect of spiritual ones.

Naturally, we fear a mugger or a murderer who can physically harm us. We should also fear those who can crush our consciences and deaden our souls. Prisoners of war and death camp survivors tell many stories about how they preserved their souls and personal integrity despite beatings, starvation, and psychological harassment. Their testimony proves the truth of Christ's axiom about the soul's resilience. We need not let anyone kill our spirits.

God is very interested in our souls which far exceed the value of a sparrow that nonetheless also engages God's attention. Worry restricts our world-view. The worrier lives in too small a world, one that excludes spiritual values. Yet, everyone in life comes one day to a moment of truth. No one is spared that moment when the challenge to act according to conscience is exacted. Worriers generally do not advert to this because their focus is on more superficial matters.

Still, what about guilt ridden and scrupulous people? Do they not worry about spiritual matters? Technically they do, but they are suffering from a greater or lesser degree of emotional upset. The object of their fear happens to be a spiritual one, but not for purposes of spiritual growth, more for liberation from emotional torment. They may need therapy more than a wisdom sermon.

The everyday worriers refuse to release themselves to work on values of character and courage. They are too timid to be brave, too delicate to be daring, too fragile to be fearless. They will not possess the spiritual resources needed to stand up for their beliefs, nor prove to be people of conscience when challenged to profess their love for Christ.

At this point Jesus introduced an observation about blasphemy of the Spirit as the unforgivable sin. This is another way of saying that the greatest sin is the conscious refusal to have faith in God. This would be based on the belief that God has nothing to do with us or for us.

Morally, this is evident in the lives of malicious, cruel, and heartless people. Amorally, this applies to those who formally repudiate all ethical and spiritual values. These are functional forms of blasphemy of the Holy Spirit that flow from a deliberate hardening of the human conscience. We cannot here examine all the circumstances that make such behavior possible, nor analyze the complex and concrete conditions that bring people to such blasphemy. (Blasphemy has also been seen as an insult to God or a sacrilegious act. Salmon Rushide's *Satanic Verses* and Martin Scorcese's *Last Temptation of Christ* fit in this category.)

Prepare for Death (Lk. 12:35-48)

Jesus carries forward his sayings about letting go of fear, but now relates them to our struggle for financial security and our need to prepare for death. This section opens with a request that Jesus arbitrate a disputed will. This is always a hornet's nest. Nothing causes more division in families than fights over money and property after the reading of a will. It does not matter if the will was that of a rich person or one of modest means. The heirs are as likely to quarrel over Uncle Henry's rocking chair as they are to dispute the dispersal of a million dollar municipal bond.

Arguments about money bring out the worst in people. Jesus refused to get involved in the argument, not because he disliked such contentiousness, but because he was more interested in spiritual maturity than financial security. This is not to say that Jesus had no desire to see that each of us have a decent way of life. He always wanted justice for all people, especially the poor. He came to bring Good News to the poor, a message of salvation from sin, but also a Gospel of a kingdom of justice and peace for all (Lk. 4:18).

Instead, here he was highlighting the truth that financial security without spiritual maturity makes little sense. That was the lesson of his story about the rich farmer who built a new barn, settled his financial affairs and sat down to enjoy his hard won prosperity. Alas, the man died at that very moment. His economic goals were legitimate, but they were insufficient. He should have been attentive to his religious future as well. Christ implied the man dealt only with his money, not his soul.

Jesus characterized that farmer as a fool. "You fool, this night your life will be demanded of you; and the things you have prepared, to whom will they belong?" (verse 20). There are rich fools who are like those who drink sea water. The more they drink, the thirstier they get. Then there are "fools for Christ," like the Philadelphia socialite Katherine Drexel. At the age of 26, she inherited a 15 million dollar fortune from her banker father. She gave up a life of luxury and ease to devote herself to the needs of Native Americans and African Americans. She founded the congregation of the Sisters of the Blessed Sacrament to fulfill her vision. Over the years, she spent 21 million dollars, which was income from the principal of her inheritance, to minister to the needs of Indians and colored people, as she would have called them in those days.

She established schools all over America for them and founded Xavier University in New orleans for the Blacks. At her death in 1955 — at the ripe old age of 95 — she could rejoice to see her congregation ministering in twenty states to thousands of her beloved people.

Jesus goes on to remind us to take a relaxed attitude toward our basic needs for food and clothing. If God feeds the birds, will he not send us food? If God cares for the lilies of the field — more splendidly arrayed than Solomon's robes — will he not care even more for us? He suggests that we have very little faith and that we spend too much time each day in a storm of stress about such matters. Why do we not trust in God who knows we need these things and so stop worrying so much?

The key to the passage is in the contrast between anxiety and faith. Jesus is not saying that we should quit our jobs or forget about prudent and responsible management of our resources and talents. By no means does he advise us to sit back while God puts money in our bank accounts, food on our table, or clothes on our backs. Perhaps the best interpretation of the text comes from St. Augustine's enlightening saying: "Act as if all depends on you. Pray as if all depends on God."

Clearly Christ expects moral and responsible behavior from us. That was the meaning of his parable of the talents. Jesus teaches that faith must be an essential aspect of this picture. Faith takes the worry out of the work. Then our work will nourish our spirituality and self worth and be an occasion for praising God.

Jesus connects his teaching about trust in divine providence to his guidelines for preparing for death (verses 32-48). In fact this trust is a form of preparation for the end. (These verses also refer to the second coming of Christ. We will treat of this theme in Luke 21:5-28).

Fear and worry dog us from the start of our conscious life until we die. We have anxiety about our survival needs and we tremble at the thought of death. Worse yet, we tend to deny our death and pretend it will not happen to us. Death afflicts other people. In our youth we operate on the myth that we are immortal — not in heaven so much as here on earth. Even after our mid-life passage, we stubbornly block out the possibility of our death. "It won't happen to me." But it will and it does.

Christ rejects this sentimentalism about death. He provides us with religious realism. "Gird your loins and light your lamps" (verse 35). Better to admit it and be like a responsible person who has cared for his or her moral and spiritual life. Preferred by far is the attitude comparable to the prudent homeowner who has safety protection for the house so that a thief will not break in.

It is not just that death will come to us, but Christ himself will come as well. He comes as a judge to evaluate our life and either welcome us to heaven or leave us to hell. These words are not meant to threaten us, so much as to invite us to care for ourselves, an act of self love which is in our best self interest, namely, our salvation. Jesus does not want to scare us, but to love us and give us the happiness which we want.

We must let go of our fear of death, so we face it clear eyed and with peaceful acceptance. Death is going home to love, to God. Our heart and soul will live forever and in a mysterious way, our bodies will share in Christ's resurrection in eternal life. We may not be able to explain this in a satisfactory manner, but we should remember this is an essential part of our faith in love and in Christ. In an age when psychological development attracts so many people, we can broaden that valid desire by affirming that our human development is completed by death in our passage to new life.

It is easy enough to identify a healthy person. What is less clear is spiritual sickness. Rosy cheeks and lean shiny bodies can hide spiritual death. In many cases the rot of evil does not show. Eventually, of course it will, because the evil of the heart will show up in destructive behavior.

When we are feeling healthy and in top form, we may pass up these words of Jesus about death and preparation. Peter thought the same way when he asked the Lord if these words applied just to others. Denial is a very old human illusion. The parable of the servants in this passage tells us that we are servants of our destiny. We have the choice to serve love and happiness in the Christian sense, or we can abdicate our responsibility. The choice is ours. The issue is clear.

Be Countercultural (Lk. 12:49-59)

Worriers and death deniers will be uncritical children of their cultures. Their anxiety makes them feel too inadequate to stand up to destructive and immoral forces in the culture. Their death denial makes them feed on the illusion that the culture is their real home even when it is evil in many ways. Freedom from worry would give them the courage to cleanse the culture. Liberation from death denial would give them an eternal perspective from which to examine and evaluate the culture.

How pale this kind of Christianity seems when viewed in the hot glow of Christ's words. "I have come to set the earth on fire, and how I wish it were already blazing!" (verse 49). Vigorous Christianity has always been a dynamic purifier of culture. If we are too worried about being liked and loved and honored by the prevailing elites in a culture, then we will never be set on fire with the passion for the justice and mercy a culture needs. From Jesus we receive the painful challenge to be "signs of contradiction." Lose the self. Take the cross. Follow Jesus.

Today's culture fosters a spirit of individualism and materialism. It instills a spirit of secularism which is a concept of a world without any need for recourse to God. Is there not a need to be counter cultural in a consumer society where the pursuit of pleasure is the supreme value, where there is too much lust for power and domination, and where there is discrimination of every kind? Ironically, this secular humanism generates inhuman attitudes. The messages from the culture disclose a number of positions alien to the teachings of Christ.

We should oppose social injustices that deprive a person of human dignity and the right to life. We ought to speak for justice for the poor and marginalized. We should join those who have a growing concern for the protection of the environment. We must uphold Christ's values about marriage and the family in the face of social evils that would destroy them, such as violence, alcoholism, drugs, child abuse, and spouse abuse.

A Christian will "set fire to the earth" by being countercultural in this sense. Jesus knows this will cause division in our families, with our friends and with the powers that be (verses 51-53). When these words were first recorded by Luke, such divisions were already occurring in the early Christian communities. We should make clear that Jesus does not want us to deliberately alienate people by coarse, insensitive, rude, abrasive words and behavior. Jesus also preached love and peace. He is simply saying that our calm, loving, compassionate, non-violent, persistent stand for Christian values will unfortunately alienate many. We will offend many. We do not need to be offensive.

To balance this, we should be just as willing to affirm the good aspects of our culture and recharge them with the power of Christ's love and grace. We do not live in a totally evil world. We must recognize the hard won beauty and values that millions espouse and work to maintain. We should celebrate technological advances that protect human dignity. We ought to rejoice in those enlightened laws, examples of progress in behavior sciences and economic systems which make human life more agreeable and creative.

This is why Jesus teaches us to read the "signs of the times" (verse 56). If we are clever enough to read the weather in the skies, should we not be more industrious in analyzing the "weather" in our culture? This skill is more important today than it was when culture was more responsive to the Christian ideals. Our secularized culture has caused the collapse of a moral consensus. The result is moral relativism, hiding in many cases behind the so-called "right to privacy."

There was a time when we could expect the culture to support our values. Today the culture often undermines them. That is why we need to read the signs of the times to see what helps us and what does not. As a Christian community, we need to pool our resources and use our collective energies to protect our families, children and society in general from forces that would cause disintegration of these essential building blocks of a culture.

In this chapter we have heard from Christ the Wisdom Speaker. Stop worrying. Prepare for death. Be countercultural. His direct and perennial wisdom has remarkable relevance for us. But then, what else is wisdom for?

Reflection

1. What is the basic difference between a prophetic preacher and a wisdom speaker?
2. We know what will kill our bodies. What are some examples of what will kill our souls?
3. Moslems say that Salmon Rushdie's *Satanic Verses* is blasphemous. From a Christian point of view, what are some similar examples of blasphemy in films, books, and plays?
4. What would I do with someone whom I perceive to be blaspheming the Holy Spirit, either refusing faith in God or actively acting without any moral conscience?
5. What "war stories" could I tell about family divisions resulting from a disputed will?
6. Why does financial security without spiritual maturity make little sense?
7. How do I balance Christ's words about being as free as the birds of the air with family responsibilities?
8. What experiences have I had of people who refuse to admit they are going to die? How did I react?
9. How could I be "counter-cultural" in my local situation?
10. How can I more effectively "read the signs of the times?"

Prayer

Jesus, eternal wisdom, you ask me to stop worrying, prepare for death, and act counter-culturally where necessary. Relax my heart. Remove from me any denial of death. Enable me to read the signs of the times. Help me to walk the razor's edge between this world and the next. Fill me with a divine perspective on life.

13 In Good Times People Play — In Bad Times They Pray

A story: A young man burst into the pastor's office saying there was an emergency at his home. His brother was in a drug frenzy and was smashing up their home with an axe. Could the priest come and help before the police arrived and arrested him? The priest left immediately and drove to the scene where the family waited outside their home. The priest went into the house and found the young man sprawled across a bed with the axe still in his hand, his eyes shut.

Praying, scared, and nervous, the priest sat by the man and offered words of hope, saying that Jesus would save him from any slavery, even one as total and terrible as drug addiction. He could not smash his own chains. He was not expected to save himself, but to turn to Jesus who came to do a job like that. Gradually, the young man let go of the axe and came in and sat down on a couch and the rest of the family came in.

Several family members began to scold him and told him what he could do to give up drugs, exactly the behavior he felt unable to do. Frustrated and feeling trapped, he rushed from the room, jumped in his car, and drove away. The priest caught up with him later and eventually things worked out, and the man was liberated from his addiction.

The lesson is that sinners who feel themselves trapped in their own weakness believe they have no place to go except down the path of self hatred and despair. Telling them what to do for themselves and how to do it, or whitewashing their guilt only adds to their frustration. The more we lecture them with self-help advice, the more they feel like giving up and even denying their freedom. We should help them turn to Jesus as one who can free them. "Truly, I say to you, everyone who commits a sin is a slave to sin. (But) if the

Son makes you free, you will be free indeed" (Jn. 8:34,36).

Turn to Jesus for Freedom from Sin (Lk. 13:1-9)

Christ's whole mission was to liberate us from all that oppresses us, above all from sin. Again and again he returned to this essential feature of his ministry as is seen in the opening of the thirteenth chapter of Luke.

Misfortune usually generates compassion for victims and their families. Yet there are times when misfortune causes people to blame the victims for their bad luck. Some hot-tempered Galileans had formed a protest demonstration at the temple during the hour of sacrifice. Luke does not cite the reason for it. Some think it was caused by Pilate's decision to use money from the temple treasury to build a new and needed aqueduct for Jerusalem. Galilean radicals would have viewed that as a provocative act. How dare he touch funds set aside for religious purposes for a public building project!

Pilate had despatched "plainclothes" soldiers to keep order. (They wore civilian cloaks over their uniforms.) Their presence as unbelievers would have been considered sacrilegious. Jews kept order with their own temple guards. Most likely, the Roman presence was discovered and fights broke out. The result was that there were "Galileans whose blood was mingled with the blood of their sacrifices" (verse 1).

Whoever brought this news to Jesus seemed to blame the Galileans for their imprudence and recklessness. They went further and hinted that their sinfulness caused their untimely deaths. Jesus did not agree with this casual judgement on the troublesome Galileans, who after all, were his own people among whom he grew up in northern Palestine. Jesus used the occasion to confront the Judeans with their own sinfulness and their need to turn to God in repentance and conversion. The possibility of a sudden and un-provided death should remind them of the state of their own moral and spiritual lives.

Jesus drove the same point home with the example of the tragic deaths of eighteen people trapped in the collapse of the Tower of Siloam. Commentators have looked in vain to confirm from extrabiblical sources the Siloam catastrophe. They have examined other histories, imperial records, governors' reports, private journals and letters from the period and found no record of it. Random disasters were always occurring then as now. Some received widespread notice. Some did not, only getting local notice. Such seems to be the case of the Siloam tragedy. Jesus selected it as another reminder of the fragility of life and the need to prepare for death by constant religious and moral conversion.

It has been said that "In good times people play and in bad times people pray." When wars come, the churches are filled. In peace and prosperity, moral fervor declines. The shock of death causes people to be reflective. Easy street dulls spiritual interests. In go-go years, the fun and games distract people from the purpose of life. When the plague comes, people wake up and wonder about the meaning of life. Jesus used the occasion of the Siloam casualties to call them to conversion and repentance.

As a master teacher, Jesus continually drew spiritual lessons from the concrete experiences of life. We have just seen how he took two news items — the murder of the Galileans and the Siloam accidental deaths — and used them as teachable moments. He reinforced his teaching on moral conversion by selecting a visual aid right before their eyes. He asked them to look at the vineyard in front of them. They saw the grape vines and also apple and fig trees planted among the vines. Good soil was so scarce that trees and vines were planted together on the same ground.

It usually took three years for a fig tree to start producing fruit. If it failed to do so, it would be cut down and replaced. Jesus took this bit of common knowledge and created a parable out of it. The owner of a vineyard inspected a three-year-old fig tree and found no fruit. He ordered it cut down because it was taking up valuable ground. The keeper of the vineyard believed the tree still had potential and argued it be given a year's grace while he nursed it along. The owner consented but warned it must be eliminated if nothing happened a year from then.

Jesus simply told the story and let it rest in the minds of his hearers. He did not apply it to their lives because he had already established the mood of the need for conversion. He let the story work its own magic on them. They saw the fig tree and heard about its life cycle. In the silence that followed the story, they could see their own lives written in that tree. For three years it would be a taker. It would breathe in the life-giving warmth of the sun. It would drink the rain and ingest the nutrients from the soil and fertilizer. It would take in all this nourishing and pampering.

After three years the tree would be expected to be a giver. If not, it would be destroyed. It might receive a year's grace because someone loved it enough to see its potential. If it still refused to be a giver, it would be destroyed. Each of us is like that fig tree. We have taken in the gifts of life and love. We prove ourselves to be spiritually and morally mature when we learn it is time to stop taking and start giving.

A Sabbath Cure (Lk. 13:10-17)

The only law that Jesus ever gave us was the law to love. By this he teaches us that all laws and rules should be at the service of loving self, neighbor, and God. At the same time, love must be more than words. Love is not very well explained by words. Only when love is translated into service does its meaning become clear. Loving behavior is the book that explains love.

Some time ago a magazine published a photo essay based on one hour of pictures of people who passed a sick man in the subway. The pictures showed people who looked at the man and then passed on without making a sympathetic inquiry. It is so easy to find reasons for deferring love.

The scene before us here is a synagogue service on the sabbath. Jesus has been invited to give the teaching. He sees a woman bent over, probably with some form of arthritis. The text says she was crippled by a spirit. Jesus himself will say that Satan held her in bondage this way for the past eighteen years. It is not important to know the medical or demonic cause of her affliction. What does count is to notice her pain and respond to it. Her sorrow touches Jesus to the point of performing a miracle to heal her.

The ruler of the synagogue complained that Jesus had broken a rule by "working" on the sabbath. He recited the reason for the no-work rule which was based on God's resting on the seventh day after six days of work in creating the world. Jesus replied by calling them hypocrites who would take their animals to watering holes on the sabbath and not consider that a breaking of sabbath rest. Is not a human being more important than an animal? Is not the relieving of human suffering an act of love that deserves to be done just as much on the sabbath as any other day? Should not the law of sabbath rest be a time for improving one's ability to love? God never rested from love. Neither should they.

What Is Christ's Kingdom Like? (Lk. 13:18-30)

The two dominant themes in Christ's preaching are salvation from sin and the kingdom (or reign) of God. What is this kingdom of God? Literally, it means the rule of God. The kingdom exists wherever God's will is being accomplished. God rules wherever his love is happening. God's loving rule is as wide as the universe, nature, history, institutions, groups, and individuals. In this sense, God's kingdom — or loving rule — embraces all existence. Wherever God's kingdom of love is acting, there is God. The kingdom of God is a saving presence through the action of the Holy Spirit of love.

The mission of the church is essentially connected to the kingdom of God, which is a kingdom of love, justice, mercy, and salvation. The church proclaims by word and sacrament the arrival of the kingdom in Jesus Christ. The members of the church, through prayer and grace, become visible witnesses of this kingdom insofar as they are transformed by the Holy Spirit. With the Spirit's power, they act out the meaning of the kingdom by loving service within the community and in the world at large.

Jesus did not speak abstractly like this about his kingdom. He wanted us to realize the kingdom was a religious truth, a spiritual mystery, but he knew how to make it concrete for his first listeners and us as well. He took a fact that everybody knows, namely, that a small seed grows into something much bigger and quite different looking than itself. Its growth process is relatively slow, invisible, and always mysterious.

Our church grew from a very tiny community into a worldwide one today over a period of 2,000 years. The small mustard seed became a big tree. The growth of the kingdom is one of remarkable power and penetration, much like a bit of yeast, even when placed in an unusually large amount of flour. Such is the manner in which the kingdom of grace penetrates and transforms the "flour" of our persons (body, spirit, emotions, and mind).

Jesus set standards for entering into the kingdom. Lose the self. Take your cross. Follow him. Believe with faith in his offer of salvation and the kingdom. Do more than obey the literal words of the commandments by fulfilling them with loving attitudes. No one should be certain that he or she has an absolute claim on the kingdom. His listeners thought they had the inside track on salvation. After all, they were God's people. They knew the laws and rules to keep as signs of their justification. They were preferred members.

Jesus took a different viewpoint. The door to the kingdom is narrow and not easy to fit through. Jesus says to the self assured, "I do not know where you come from. Depart from me you evildoers!" (verse 27).

There will be surprises for complacent people. Think of the story of the woman who was accustomed to all kinds of comfort and luxury. She died and went to heaven. An angel greeted her and took her to her new home. They passed all kinds of beautiful mansions. As they came to each one, the woman thought that one would be hers. In time they came to a small dwelling on the outskirts of the heavenly city. It was barely a shack. "This is your place," said the angel. The woman shouted in great disappointment, "That! I could never live there!" "Sorry," said the angel, "but that is the best we could do with the materials you sent us."

We tend to justify ourselves with thoughtless behavior. So much of it is so unreflective and unthinking, that we imagine that is all that Jesus expects of us. It is not that Jesus expects us to do great things, but that he wants us to do little things with great love. Instead we drift, saying, "We ate and drank in your company. You taught us in your streets" (verse 26). The implication is that we are so self-satisfied with our routine Christianity that we never stop to realize that we hold our souls in our hands and need to have a more conscious view of our destinies. Heaven is not an automatic reward for mere membership in the church or mere abstinence from immorality. That is too negative. Jesus will judge us not just on what we omitted, but the love we have committed.

Through baptism and faith, we enter the door of the kingdom here on earth. But we are not all the way in. That will happen only in heaven. During this earthly testing period, we can fall away. Worse yet, we can delude ourselves that we are still in the kingdom when our selfishness and lack of attentiveness threaten to cancel our membership even here.

Herod's Threat (Lk. 13:31-33)

Some friendly Pharisees came to Jesus and warned him that Herod may try to kill him just as he did John the Baptist. A special value of this passage is that it shows there were Pharisees who admired Jesus. Not all of them were the hostile hypocrites who normally appear in the gospel accounts.

Herod's threat did not intimidate Jesus or distract him from his goal. He calls Herod a fox, but one that is not sly enough to change Christ's firm plans for salvation. Jesus says he must continue on his chosen path to die in Jerusalem.

Lament Over Jerusalem (Lk. 13:34-35)

Jesus loved his holy city of Jerusalem. He loved its people. But he lamented the history of its leaders who have constantly persecuted and killed the prophets. This did not cool his affection for Jerusalem which he compared to a mother hen's love for her children. Augustine carried this picture further. "With her wings drooping, her feathers ruffled, her voice hoarse, in all her limbs she becomes so sunken and depressed that even if you cannot see her young, you can see she is a mother. This is the way Jesus feels" (*Commentary on John's Gospel*, 15, 7). Jesus loves her even though he foresees her leaders rejecting and killing him, just as she did with the prophets.

Reflection

1. What do I notice about people's sense of personal sin today?
2. People asked Jesus if he thought the radical Galileans were murdered because they were sinful. How would I have answered them?
3. What are some examples today of blaming the victim for his or her misfortunes?
4. What stories can I tell about the fragility of life?
5. What value do I experience in preparing for my death?
6. How would I apply Christ's parable of the fig tree to my life?
7. How would I explain that religious laws are ways to love self, others, and God?
8. What does Christ's teaching on the kingdom of God mean to me?
9. How do the parables of the mustard seed and the leaven make sense today?
10. Why did Jesus weep over Jerusalem?

Prayer

Savior of the world, you have offered me salvation from all that would oppress me, above all from my sins. Help me to have a true and honest appreciation of the moral and spiritual state of my life. Assist me to be honest in evaluating myself and my behavior in the light of your teachings and expectations. Strengthen me with the love of the Holy Spirit and your gift of the Sacrament of Reconciliation.

14   The Meals of St. Luke

"When you hold a banquet, invite the poor" (verse 13). Oscar Schindler was a wonderful example of a man who served the poor and oppressed. This Roman Catholic industrialist became an angel to the Jews headed for death camps in World War II. He did not appear to be an angel. Externally, he seemed to be a self-indulgent man. He dressed fashionably, chain smoked, kept a wife and a mistress and a garage full of expensive cars. In 1939 he took over a bankrupt enamelware factory in Cracow and struck it rich with war contracts.

One day Oscar drove by a Jewish ghetto and saw Nazis with rampaging dogs murdering Jews at random. The scene converted him. He resolved to defeat the system and help the Jews. He approached the SS captain who was creating a forced labor camp. The captain loved to beat up women and shoot men for walking too slowly. He stole ghetto food and resold it for profit on the black market. Schindler gave him cognac and gold and persuaded him to let the Jews live at his factory. Oscar spent $120,000 turning his factory into a camp for Jews. He spent $10,000 a month to feed them.

When the Nazis decided to exterminate the Jews, Schindler planned to save them. He bought another factory and persuaded the Nazis to let him ship Jews there. The 800 men on his list went first. Three hundred women were diverted to Auschwitz. Oscar went there and rescued those freezing, starved, and desperate women. He loaded them on a box car which the Nazis thought was going to another death camp. When the terrified women came out of the car, they saw Oscar. "You're safe now. You're with me."

This angel of God's poor lived an uneventful life after the war. He died in 1974 and was mourned by "Schindler Jews" all over the world. He is buried in Jerusalem. When the Allies liberated his factory in Moravia, his workers presented him with a ring made from the gold bridgework of one man's teeth. Inside was an engraving from the Talmud. "He who saves a single life saves the world." His inspiring story echoes Christ's emphasis on love for the poor so often found in the meal stories of Luke.

Meal Stories in St. Luke (Lk. 14:1-24)

The fourteenth chapter of Luke begins with three accounts about meals. All the gospels stress the importance of meals with Jesus, but none surpasses their significance in Luke as Father Eugene La Verdiere has often pointed out. Meal stories appear in every section of Luke from the first dinner in Levi's house to the apostles' fish dinner with Christ after Easter. These dining situations become occasions for Jesus to honor table fellowship and use the events as teachable moments.

Meals of Gospel Values. Christ's dining practices produced criticisms. Pharisees complained that he ate with tax collectors and sinners. They wondered why his disciples did not fast like those of John the Baptist. They objected to his refusal to follow the washing rituals that were expected at a meal. They criticized him for healing the man with dropsy at a sabbath meal, a day in which such "work" was forbidden. Jesus used these eating occasions to illustrate his gospel values: reconciliation with sinners; joy in the advent of salvation; the superior importance of cleansing the soul more than hand washings; the primacy of love as the substance of the sabbath.

Meals of Christian Behavior. In other dining events, Jesus explained what it meant to have table fellowship with him and what this would signify for the Christian mission. For those who fussed about details, as Martha did, Jesus emphasized the essentials of Christianity. When he saw people angling for the places of honor at table, he said that humility was better. They should seek the lowest place, for the humble will be exalted and the proud will be humbled.

Noticing that his hosts loved to have important people at their meals for personal advancement, he taught that they should invite the poor, the blind, and the lame who could not repay them with fancy dinners. Love and compassion is its own reward, for every act of love given is already received. It was at suppers that Jesus appealed for Christian attitudes suitable for those who are members of the kingdom of God.

When Jesus wanted to enliven the missionary vision of his

apostles, he told them not to send people home to eat, but to nourish them. He demonstrated this teaching with his miracle of the bread. At the Last Supper, when the apostles argued about who would be greatest among them, Jesus admonished them to worry more about serving people than controlling them with power. "For who is greater: the one seated at table or the one who serves? Is it not the one seated at table? I am among you as the one who serves" (Lk. 22:27).

Meals of Faith Experience. In one of the loveliest of all gospel stories, the Emmaus narrative, Jesus chose a meal to reveal his risen presence to two disciples. During the Emmaus journey, Jesus nourished their faith, preparing the ground for later belief. Because of their newly awakened faith, they were able to see his real presence in the breaking of the bread.

The next day Jesus met with all the apostles. They were startled and afraid, thinking they saw a ghost. Jesus reassured them that he was their friend, a real human being who had flesh and bones which could be touched. To reinforce for them the reality of his risen body, he asked them for food. They served him a meal of baked fish. This is the way Jesus evoked from them a faith in the total reality of his resurrection. Moreover, by asking them for food, he illustrated that in the future he would come to them in the hungry and the poor. It was like telling them, "I receive your hospitality today when you see me here. In the future I will meet you in the guise of a poor and hungry person. Be as ready to feed and love me then as you do now."

Meals for the Poor. Hunger and lack of food is the perennial sign of being poor. The Christian meal was supposed to be a time of sharing food and fellowship. In an ideal Christian community, no one should be hungry. Acts 2:42-47 seems to indicate there was generous sharing at Christian meals. But as the Christian community developed, the problems Jesus noted at his meals arose again. Annanias and Sapphira ceased to share and instead hoarded their money and trusted more in power and prestige.

In time the work of the ministry required the creation of deacons so that someone would be sure to see that everyone was fed. "The widows were being neglected in the daily distribution" (Acts 6:1). We know that the deacons went on to preach and evangelize, but their original ministry was to the poor and hungry — a ministry that all Christians should still follow.

Reconciling Meals. Jesus chose meals to dramatize his desire to be reconciled with sinners and tax collectors such as Matthew and Zaccheus. In the story of the Prodigal Son, Jesus shows that the reluctance of the older brother to attend the reconciliation meal for his younger brother is not kingdom behavior. The father's appeal to the older son to be more forgiving and reconciling touched the listeners of the early Christian community just as much as it does today.

We have placed this extended reflection on the meals of Jesus in Luke's gospel because this fourteenth chapter starts off with three meal accounts. It seemed to be the best time to focus on the importance of meal narratives in Luke and to see their religious meaning and teaching. This reflection should provide a sufficient commentary on these three stories which so insistently show how Jesus used meal experiences for gospel purposes.

It should also be noted that virtually all these observations also apply to our understanding of the Holy Eucharist. This is the unsurpassable sacrificial meal of salvation, reconciliation, prayer, and humility. This is the sacrament that offers us the gifts of Christian attitudes and behaviors, especially concern for the poor, the hungry, and the dispossessed.

More on Discipleship (Lk. 14:25-33)

Jesus returns again to his teachings about the meaning of discipleship. Using oriental exaggeration, he says that one must be capable of hating one's own family in order to follow him. This has never been understood as a literal "hating" for Jesus has always made love the essential act of all followers. His picturesque saying was meant to illustrate the depth of commitment to him that discipleship demanded.

We have already seen that there are times when one's Christian behavior may alienate friends and family who either do not understand or accept it. Clearly, our purpose is not to create family animosity, but rather to be true to one's conscience in following Jesus. Even when such alienation occurs, we should always keep the lifeline open, be ever willing to love, and be reconciled to family and friends when that becomes possible.

Jesus then repeats his abiding principle of the cross as an essential feature of discipleship. Here he states it negatively. Whoever does not take up the cross cannot be a disciple. Christian discipleship will not result from "cheap grace," or the easy path. It will always be associated with "costly grace," the royal road of the cross.

Basically, Jesus tells us that Christian life will be difficult. This is one of the greatest truths that Jesus taught us. Most of us do not like to hear this part of his message. We want Christian life to be easy. Whenever it gets hard we moan and complain. We criticize someone — often church authorities — for making religion difficult. We cry out that we are not supposed to have such a hard time being a Christian.

We claim that we are being victimized and we turn against others for persecuting us, often when they have nothing to do with it. We pay so much attention to our own hurts that we fail to see that Christian life inevitably includes tragedy, disappointment, suffering, and pain. In fact, all life does, Christian or otherwise. Supreme realist that he is, Jesus reminds us that discipleship will involve pain and there is no avoiding it. We will not like it.

Only when we are willing to face the cross and take it will we begin to grow as Christian disciples. The cross will make us feel uncomfortable. The pain of confronting and accepting our cross causes us to think of ways to avoid it. Instead of relieving our discomfort, the avoidance only plunges us more deeply into a limbo of frustration. Only when we face and accept the cross Jesus gives us will we begin to experience peace and joy. This is the whole point of our act of faith, for it alone enables us to take the cross and experience the consequent joy.

This is not the same as masochism which is the seeking of pain for its own sake. We do not need to seek pain. It is there already in our lives. It is not a question of seeking, but of getting over avoiding what is offered to us. Fearing the pain of the cross causes escapism in us. This escapism may occur in drugs, alcohol, and sex which are major ways to dull the ache, but do not succeed. The true road to spiritual wholeness — holiness — is the honest acceptance of the cross which appears to us in the various troubles, aches, and pains of ordinary life. It also comes in the form of temptations to choose the paths of sin and evil as methods to avoid the challenge of the cross and the peace and happiness which it alone can bring.

Though we hate to hear it, Jesus tells us that suffering is both necessary and valuable for the total growth of our personhood. This is really Gospel — Good News — though it appears to be at first sight bad news to us and certainly in the eyes of the "feel-good culture." Christ actually does want us to feel good, but only through the reality therapy of the carrying of the cross, for that is the only true way to enduring happiness and inner peace. We must face the cross and experience the pain involved.

Jesus has given us a whole series of methods for facing and carrying our crosses. His eight beatitudes (four of them in Luke and eight in Matthew) and his Sermon on the Mount (Sermon on the Plain in Luke) are the major guidelines for how to face and carry a cross. The lessons he gave at meals, just reviewed above, are amplifications of his methods for cross carrying. Luke has summarized them in a triple formula: Lose the self. Take the cross. Follow Jesus.

We have only two choices, to take and carry the cross or to refuse and avoid it. In the second choice we do not really avoid pain and suffering, we run deeper into it and suffer helplessly with no easing of the pain or turning our sorrows into joy.

We think the two worst things that can happen to us are the loss of self and death. To even hint that this is a good idea is to utter a cruel joke especially in a world that glamorizes the fulfillment of self and the denial of death. Only in the losing of self can we find the lasting and durable joy we want to have. Only in admitting, facing and taking on the reality of our death, do we overcome it through Christ's resurrection.

The wisdom of the ages has always connected death and rebirth, especially among cultures that were close to the life cycles of agrarian life. What Jesus invites us to in his call to discipleship is elevation of the death and rebirth cycle to the Christian way. The cross is in reality the series of mini-deaths we can experience on our life journey. These small deaths lead to an ever increasing series of rebirths that account for our personal happiness and designate the increasing depth of our capacity to love self, others, and God.

The saints have always known the value of this process and reveal its value to us in numerous ways. One of the reasons they talk so much about discipline is that they have found this is the only way to be a disciple, a word that is essentially related to discipline. It takes discipline to be a disciple, because it takes discipline to open oneself to the experience of the cross. Without discipline we will run away from the unpleasantness of the cross and the uncomfortable feelings it gives us. Discipline pulls us together and keeps us from avoiding the cross. This would be more difficult without faith and love in Christ. But with such faith and love, we will conquer all, even death itself.

Reflection

1. What are the most important meals for me and my family? Why?
2. What does a good meal symbolize for me?
3. How did Jesus make a meal an occasion for teaching Gospel values?
4. In the Prodigal Son story, why does the refusal of the older brother to attend the meal in honor of his younger brother seem so un-Christian?
5. What are some stories I could tell about people using meals for ego trips?
6. What is the connection between the Christian view of a meal and Christian concern for the poor and hungry?
7. What connection can be seen between the meals of Jesus in the gospel and the Holy Eucharist?
8. How does Jesus take the inevitable sufferings of life and relate them to discipleship?
9. What are some ways that people use to avoid the cross?
10. What is the link between discipline and discipleship?

Prayer

Jesus, host of the many meals of the gospel, especially of the Last Supper, you teach us that at these dining experiences, we can learn many of the Gospel values you want us to have. Above all, in the Eucharist, we celebrate your sacrificial presence and table fellowship. May our beliefs, attitudes, and practices reflect our communion with you, both in the Sacrament and in our daily behavior.

15 Lost Sheep, Lost Coin, Lost Son

There is a spiritual technique known as the "Parade of the Night" in which the participants pass before their minds' eyes all the faces of the people they met that day. As each face appears, the people review what their interaction was with the pictured persons.

Did I treat the person carelessly? Did I act in a patronizing manner? Was I putting on a show to impress the other? Did I pretend to be friendly to cover up my hostility? Was I afraid of the person? Did I try to make the person feel at ease and be happy? Was I generous with my time?

The "Parade of the Night" helps me evaluate how I treat people, how I make Christ's kingdom practical in my relationships with others. Love remains an abstraction until I put it into action by serving others. How narrow is the door to my heart? How defensive am I in reacting to others? How open should I be? How easily do I realize that Jesus comes to me in each person I meet, offering me an opportunity for affection and compassionate action.

In chapter fifteen of Luke, we read a parade of three parables that open up the mind's eye to see three different ways of practicing kingdom behavior.

Take Time for the Lost Sheep and the Lost Coin (Lk. 15:1-10)

Over ninety percent of the church's resources are poured into parish and diocesan maintenance. In terms of Christ's parable of the Lost Sheep, most of the church's funds and energies are directed to the "ninety-nine" sheep, meaning the active membership, and relatively little devoted to the lost sheep.

Who are the lost sheep today? In the United States they are the ninety million people who are either inactive members of their churches or they are simply the unchurched — belonging to no denomination. In the world at large, the lost sheep are the several billion people who have not yet been offered the opportunity to hear the Good News of Jesus Christ and been invited to accept his saving love and membership in the church.

Vatican II's document on missionary activity (*Ad Gentes*) urged a renewed effort to evangelize the world, to reach the lost sheep. In 1976, Pope Paul VI wrote an enthusiastic apostolic exhortation on the critical need for evangelizing the world. Pope John Paul II has declared the 1990's to be the decade of evangelization in preparation for the third millennium of Christianity in the year 2000. He has amplified his call by his encyclical, *The Mission of the Redeemer* (*Missio Redemptoris*). The 500th anniversary of the advent of Christianity to the New World constitutes another awareness experience related to evangelization.

Because of this, the idea that all Christians should be more active in sharing their faith both with each other and those who do not yet know Jesus has occurred. Looking for the lost sheep today means renewing the missionary commitment of each Christian. Faith is strengthened when it is given to others. More important is the benefit to others. Evangelization is a service that advances human dignity and freedom. It honors and enriches local cultures and respects what is valued in every religion. This legitimate respect for cultures and religions must not deter us from making the case for Christ who will bring even greater beauty to these cultures and religions.

Closer to home, who would be the lost sheep among Catholics? This is the inactive Catholic, a person who goes to church at Christmas and Easter, for weddings and funerals, for Ashes and Palms (the "A&P Catholic") and two other times.

Gallup and Castelli characterize inactive Catholics this way:

1. Ancestral Catholics. Two million people identify themselves as Catholics even though they have never belonged to the church. Parental affiliation accounts for this. They should be willing candidates for evangelization since they profess Catholic identity and have not formally left or drifted away from the church.

2. Ambiguous Catholics. Eleven million people say they are Catholics even though they seldom go to Mass more than four times

a year. They tend to move in and out of active membership without changing their sense of identity. Many of these would respond positively to an invitation to "come home."

3. "We Left" Catholics. Four million Catholics say they have formally left the church, yet, nearly two million of these have a warm spot for the church and have thought of returning. This is an encouraging sign for evangelizers.

Catholic University's Dean Hoge lists five kinds of Catholic dropouts — or lost sheep.

1. Family Tension Dropouts — 24%. These persons experienced tensions in their parental families. As soon as they could, they rebelled against both family and church. This usually happens when they leave home or their parents have reduced their pressures. Twenty-four percent.

2. Weary Dropouts — 31%. These persons found the church boring and uninteresting. They lacked motivation for Mass attendance. Sometimes the motivation they once had evaporated — loss of a churchgoing spouse or when the children left home.

3. Lifestyle Dropouts — 23%. These persons objected to Catholic moral teachings and feared going to confession. Some were divorced or had lifestyles in conflict with the church's moral teachings.

4. Spiritual Need Dropouts — 7%. These persons experienced a void in spiritual needs not met by the church. In their distress they stayed away from the church or joined some other religious group.

5. Anti-Change Dropouts — 7%. These persons objected to changes in the Mass and other changes in their parishes. They preferred the old style Latin Mass and felt uneasy with liturgical innovations. (Cf. Dean Hoge's *Converts, Dropouts, Returnees*, United States Catholic Conference publication, 1981.)

In his parable of the Lost Sheep, Jesus shows us the three elements that form our strategy for reaching the lost sheep. First, trust that the "ninety-nine" are not going to disappear by paying some attention to evangelization. The fact of the matter is that evangelizing parishes grow. Studies show that American denominations that have abandoned evangelization have lost nearly a third of their active membership.

Second, be convinced of the need to share our faith with those who have drifted away or formally rejected the church. We must believe that evangelizing is part of our baptismal commitment. This does not mean a religious imperialism whereby we force our faith down others' throats. This is not a muscular proselytizing that intimidates or shames others into joining the church. Our style must be invitational, loving, affectionate. We need to believe that Jesus Christ is intrinsically appealing because of his love, beauty, wonder, and inherent attractiveness. No one needs to be compelled to enjoy and take a rose. They just need to know and experience the rose. It is the same with Jesus.

Thirdly, this should be done with joy and lightness of heart. We do not need the stern pose of the debater, or the lusty militancy of a hunter. We need not huff and puff to blow down the defenses of the lost sheep. The Holy Spirit is the strong and gentle persuader who does the real work, so long as we have the faith, kindness, and willingness to extend an inviting hand to the lost sheep.

In this regard, Jesus uses another image dear to the heart of everyone who has lost his or her wallet. Nothing stirs our search impulses more than our frantic effort to find a lost wallet with its money, drivers license, and credit cards. This is our version of the "lost coin" of the gospel. We all know the anxiety we feel when we have mislaid our wallets, especially when vacationing away from home. American Express has capitalized on that fear with its ads for express checks: "Don't leave home without them."

Jesus sympathizes with us in our predicament and rejoices with us when we find our wallets, just as the lady found her coin. But Christ's point drives deeper. This search and its happy outcome is an image of our call to evangelize those who have drifted away from Christ and the church and the subsequent joy that comes from bringing someone home. "There will be rejoicing among the angels of God over one sinner who repents" (verse 10). This leads Jesus to tell one of his greatest parables, the story of the Lost Son.

The Prodigal Son and the Prodigal Father (Lk. 15:11-32)

The story line of this parable is about the younger of two brothers who asks his father for his inheritance. Upon receiving it, he traveled to a foreign country where he wasted all his money on foolish and sinful pleasures. Totally broke, he found himself in a country that suffered from financial depression due to a famine. A swineherd gave him a job tending the pigs. So small were his wages that he could not buy enough food to feed himself. He yearned to eat the food given to the pigs but was not allowed to.

Hitting rock bottom he came to his senses, realizing that his father's workers had plenty to eat and he was starving. He decided to go home, apologize to God and his father for his sins, declare he was unworthy to be called his father's son, and ask for a job on the estate.

Meanwhile the father deeply missed his young son. Each day he stood on a hill full of compassion for the boy and hoping he would come home. Then he saw his son coming toward him. He ran to his son, hugged and kissed him, and praised God for his return. With tears of joy and much embracing, the father smothered the repentant words of his son. The father jubilantly called out to the servants to clothe his son in the best robe, put a ring on his finger and sandals on his feet. He ordered the fattened calf to be slaughtered and roasted for a feast. Why? "This son of mine was dead and has come to life again. He was lost and has been found" (verse 24).

The older son heard the commotion and asked what it was about. When he heard the reason he was furious. Pouting, he refused even to enter the house. The father came out and pleaded with him to come inside and celebrate the homecoming of his younger brother. The older one argued that the young tramp did not deserve this. He had wasted his inheritance on prostitutes and wild living. Why should he, who had been the good and faithful son and never had a party like this given in his honor, be humiliated by sitting in the glory given to this good-for-nothing sinner?

The father replied that the older son had absolute security and the utmost respect of his father. Everything the father owned belonged to him. "Be forgiving and generous hearted. Your brother was dead and is risen again. Rejoice in his return to grace and this home of love!"

The story contains several important symbols. The younger son represents each one of us in our sinfulness. The father symbolizes God as a loving and forgiving person. The older son stands for the human unwillingness to forgive, even when repentance has been expressed.

Usually the story is named after the prodigal son who wasted all his wealth and sinned deeply. But the narrative just as well could be called the parable of the Prodigal God who spends his vast wealth of forgiveness more prodigiously than any sinner exhausts his life and earnings. If human sin abounds, God's love abounds more.

If this forgiveness is to be received, we must overcome denial of our sinfulness. Admitting our poverty and powerlessness is very hard on our pride and difficult in a culture that prizes power and pretense. Many of us have made a mess of our lives and are powerless to change our present situations. We have learned to put on a front that hides our problems both from ourselves, our families and our society.

Our culture favors the denial of sin. Our society seems to say we should live "no fault lives." As a community we must take moral responsibility for eradicating this false view of life. At the same time, we suffer individually from this delusion. "It's not my fault. There is nothing wrong. I have not sinned." The individual, however, must take responsibility for personal behavior. "This is my life. It has reached a point of being unmanageable." The young man of the parable reached this insight and was able to find a way to turn his life around.

The next step is to look for a power that will liberate us from the insanity and powerlessness that grips us in our sins. This requires that we have faith in the possibility of being freed from what enslaves us. We must believe that there is a love stronger than the death of sin. We should believe there is a loving person who will walk with us through the fears and negative feelings that sin generates. To our lips will come the words of confession, perhaps with apprehension for our trust is weak, but firm nonetheless because we have nowhere else to turn. The prodigal son knew his father was just such a person. In our lives we can come to Jesus who grandly fulfills the kindness and affection we will need as we seek forgiveness.

The encounter with forgiveness is far more liberating and joyful than prior fears could imagine. Christ does not linger on our apologies. These are necessary for us so we can verify that we have overcome the state of unhealthy denial. Jesus knows what is in our hearts before the words reach our lips. But we often do not, hence, our confession means a great deal for our own integrity. We soon discover that Christ's attitude of acceptance made possible our outreach to him for reconciliation. It is not that our confession wins his forgiveness. It is Christ's forgiveness that makes our confession possible.

Humanly speaking, this makes little sense to a culture that denies sin. Moreover on the human level, even religiously correct people fail to see the point. They have reduced religion to a balanced contract between services offered and rewards obtained. Cloaking this process with religious justifications only confuses the situation and hides the real miracle of religion, the encounter of divine forgiveness that causes humble repentance.

This is a love contract not a business one. The older brother was a good man in human terms. He was diligent, faithful to duty, and bore the heat of the day. But his virtue was barren because it was inflated with human self justification. He simply could not forgive his brother no matter how much he repented. He misunderstood the whole point of religion which was meant to transform him into a gracious and forgiving person. He did not possess the virtue of faith. He relished only his self righteousness. His strength did not reside in God. His power derived from his own small world-view, a vision that trapped him into a sour and uncompromising judgementalism.

The story of the prodigal son invites us to ask ourselves three questions. Am I a person who is intolerant and unforgiving of the faults and sins of others? Am I a person who has messed up my life and is now ready to trust in a power higher than myself to save me? Do I really believe in a God whose loving forgiveness makes possible my conversion and repentance? The parable shows us the answers to these questions and the victory of the spirit that is available to us.

Reflection

1. When I tried the spiritual technique of the "Parade of the Night," what did it do for me?
2. Why would a parish fear to use some of its resources to find the lost sheep?

3. What are some signs that the church has a renewed interest in evangelization of the lost sheep?
4. What blocks do I run into personally when I consider my own vocation to evangelize?
5. Hoge and Gallup-Castelli have listed various kinds of lost sheep. Which ones have I met?
6. Are there "prodigal sons" in my family or among my acquaintances?
7. What examples do I have in my experience of unforgiving people (the older brother of the story)?
8. If my culture teaches me to deny sin, what should I do about it?
9. If the first step in repentance is acknowledgement of my sins, what is my next step?
10. What experiences have I had of loving and forgiving people whose attitudes have enabled conversion and repentance of others?

Prayer

Forgiving Jesus, your love has moved you to seek the lost sheep, the lost coin, the lost son and daughter. You show us the importance of evangelizing so that others may experience your love. You urge me to have a reconciling spirit that favors repentance in others. With the power of your Spirit I will open myself to these attitudes and behaviors.

16   Imitate Both the Clever and the Merciful

The Clever Manager (Lk. 16:1-13)

Like any imaginative teacher, Jesus ransacked the nooks and crannies of his culture to find examples to illustrate his points. He understood the power of a story to capture a listener's attention and found material for his stories sometimes in the most unlikely places. His tale of the clever manager is a case in point.

An employer found out that the manager of his properties was wasting money and mishandling the affairs of the estate. He notified the manager about his displeasure and demanded a formal accounting of his stewardship. The manager realized he was in deep trouble and decided he must do something to protect his future. He visited all the debtors of his employer. He told them he was reducing their debts by up to fifty percent and fixing the financial ledgers accordingly. Believing this act would win him friends among those whose debts he lowered, the manager felt more secure about his future.

The employer discovered how his manager had cheated him. Logically the story should say at this point that the wildly angry employer reamed out his manager, charged him with tampering with financial records, and notified the debtors there would be lawsuits if they did not pay what they owed. Instead Jesus introduces a startling twist in the tale. He has the employer congratulating the cheating manager for his cleverness in securing his own future.

On the surface this is a troubling conclusion. How can a great moral teacher like Jesus seem to approve an immoral and illegal act? Surely Jesus cannot support the action of a liar and a thief. The Christ who stood for truth, honesty, and justice could hardly be changing his mind here by praising a criminal act. Nor would he be simply displaying a sly sense of humor, noting how shrewdly a rascal can outwit his rich master, acting as a Robin Hood on his own behalf by taking from the rich to fill his own poor future.

What then was Jesus driving at? The key is found in his statement that worldly people are shrewder than religious people. What he means is that the children of the world are more imaginative than the children of faith in pursuing their goals. Today he would be saying that secular-minded people possess more creative energy in getting what they want than faith people do in advancing the kingdom of love, justice, and peace.

Jesus is not approving the deception of the clever manager, but he is holding up for Christians the example of his inventiveness and energy in achieving his goals. If wicked people can be so energetic in making evil happen, why can't faith people be even more creative in making the kingdom happen?

This interpretation applies equally to Christ's advice to "make friends with dishonest wealth" (verse 9). He asked his first listeners — and us as well — to study the drive, enthusiasm, originality, intelligence, wit, and cleverness of people whose goals are purely materialistic. Their example of unremitting pursuit of becoming rich and famous should shame us into being even better and more committed to achieving the goals of a moral and spiritual character and destiny.

Jesus concluded his story with the hard-headed observation that one cannot serve two masters. We will either hate one and love the other, be devoted to one and reject the other. Shrewd observer of human behavior that he was, Jesus struck home with this rock hard wisdom teaching. "You cannot serve God and mammon" (verse 13). This saying dispels all confusion, lest there be any doubt of what he meant by his parable. Jesus is not endorsing evil behavior. He has used the story to show that secularist people can be superior to religious ones in using every waking moment to accomplish their purposes.

Some have said that sin is a form of laziness. People are not inclined to make the effort to resist evil Nor do they pull themselves together enough to act out of love This is true in its own way, but we should see now that sin itself demands its own "work ethic" as in the case of thriving materialists. The nugget of truth in the saying that sin is a form of laziness is that it takes more energy to be virtuous than to be sinful. The clever manager was not lazy, but Christ's listeners were. He tells them and us that we must abandon the laziness that puts off our day of reckoning when we decide to serve God instead of mammon.

The Rich Man and Lazarus (Lk. 16:19-31)

Jesus then told his wonderful story about the rich man and Lazarus. A self-indulgent rich man feasted every day. A poor man named Lazarus sat at the door of the mansion and ate the garbage from the rich man's table. Dogs licked the poor man's sores. When Lazarus died, he went to heaven (in the bosom of Abraham). The rich man died and went to hell. The tormented rich man asked Father Abraham to let Lazarus cool his tongue with a drop of water. Abraham said it could not be done. The gulf between them was impassable.

The rich man asked that Lazarus be permitted to visit his five living brothers so they would not succumb to this fate. Abraham said they have the teachings of Moses and the prophets. The rich man said they will listen better to those doctrines if a man risen from the dead tells them. Abraham said that if they were not open to God's word now, a man come back from the dead will not convince them. People against their will are of the same opinion still.

The rich man wanted mercy after he died. But he showed no mercy while he was alive. The secret of obtaining mercy is to give it during the time of our human development here. Jesus taught, "Blessed are the merciful for they shall obtain mercy" (Mt. 5:7). The rich man did not have a social conscience. He had no interest in the political and economic causes of hunger and homelessness. Worse yet he did not even have the sensitivity to notice the misery of a homeless and hungry person at his doorstep.

Self absorbed, he paid no attention to the needs of others. His belly was warm with food and his heart cheered by wine. Rich enough to indulge himself, he cared little about the nourishing of his conscience. It never occurs to him to show mercy. Because he has never given mercy, he cannot receive any. It is only in the giving of mercy that it can be received.

The first step in having a social conscience is to have a sensitivity to the person in need we meet in daily life. A compassionate awareness of the effects of injustice will move us to correct the causes of injustice. Healing the symptoms of injustice leads to healing the causes of poverty, misery, and unfairness. Being an angel of mercy is the first step on the road to becoming a prophet of justice.

If we want to test our capacity for love, we should examine how well we bring the warmth of mercy to those in need. Mercy is both an expression of love and a pre-condition for bringing justice to our community. The merciful receive mercy even when it seems to be a one-way street. A doctor treating his patients with compassion is already increasing his capacity for compassion. A parent who treats a child tenderly has just received a new abundance of personal tenderness. A benefactor who educates a poor student receives an even more generous spirit from the deed.

Jesus taught that whatever we have done to another, we have done to him. Christ accepts this as though it were shown to himself. This fact calls us to sharpen continually our purposes in all we do. We must grow in awareness of what is going on in relating to others. Consciously treating others with compassion means we are immediately acting toward Jesus in that moment — and thereby receiving a new infusion of compassion for ourselves. If we would like to be known as compassionate people, then we must give compassion to others. The gift of compassion stretches our souls the very moment we act compassionately.

In terms of the parable, Jesus, in the person of Lazarus, sat at the door of the rich man's house, offering him the daily opportunity to receive a gift that far surpassed his wealth and richly laden table. But materialism blinded the perception of the rich man so much so that he did not even advert to the hungry and homeless man at his door. So dull was his conscience that he no longer saw a problem. In the laziness of his sin, he sank into the cushions of his dining room and let alcohol numb his brain and fat foods weigh down his body. The result was a dead soul that would one day cry for mercy when it was too late.

Mercy enhances the sense of equality between people when it is performed with Christ's view of the act. Some people think of mercy as a transaction in which a superior person (rich and powerful) takes time to do a "good deed" for an inferior person. This has rightly been criticized as a patronizing approach. Critics say that justice is the better way.

Jesus did not see mercy or justice in that light. In his view, justice is equality brought about in the exterior world of a fair distribution of goods and services to all people. But mercy is an equality based upon interior similarity of dignity and humanity. Mercy is the soul of justice. St. Paul articulated Christ's teaching about this when he wrote, "If I give away everything that I own . . . so that I may boast. but do not have love, I gain nothing" (I Cor. 13:3).

First we must love the people we help. Loving mercy reveals the human dignity of the other person, who is not only just as good as we are, but may be spiritually deeper in fact, (Lazarus, recall, went to heaven). It equalizes our relationship in our common humanity and opens us to receive from the person we help the gift of mercy in return. Perhaps that is what St. Vincent De Paul meant when he advised a young novice, "You must love the poor so they can forgive you for what you offer them."

Merciful love does more than anything else to establish a mutual relationship with others based on reverence and respect for the human dignity of another. Whatever justice we shall be called to bring about in the world will need the corrective warmth of a love that is patient and kind. When this kind of love exists between husbands and wives, parents and children, the neighbors in our community, the people at the office or factory, then it will trickle upward to the leaders of nations, businesses, universities, and other institutions. The rich man failed to see this. Lazarus saw it only too well. The story challenges our deepest perceptions of ourselves and our relationships. Clearly, we know what we should do.

Reflection

1. Do I know of people who use a lot of imagination and energy to make money and achieve fame? Discuss.
2. What was Christ trying to tell me in the story of the clever manager?

3. From the stories that I hear about inventive materialists, what can I learn about my spiritual growth?
4. What do I think of when I hear that sin is a form of laziness?
5. How can sin be a type of laziness when so many sinners seem enthusiastic and energetic about their immoral goals?
6. In my honest moments, do I think that the hungry and the homeless are inferior to me? If so what causes this?
7. How is it possible that I receive mercy in giving mercy?
8. How does a true act of compassion reveal to me the equality of the other person with myself?
9. Why is it true to say that mercy is the soul of justice?
10. How does mercy lead me to advocate justice?

Prayer

Dear Jesus, imaginative and merciful, you open me to see how much creativity I need to be your disciple and how much mercy I must show to act as a disciple. Urge me to be more imaginative in growing spiritually than worldly people are in their quest for materialistic triumphs. Invite me more urgently to learn your basic guideline about giving mercy in order to receive it. Make me a just and merciful person.

17 The Seven Stages of Temptation

The Temptation Process (Lk. 17:1-10)

Temptation is the process that leads to sin. The gospels reflect what is most real in human life. That is why they report stories and sayings about sin, evil, and temptation, the negative aspect of life. We so deeply associate love, hope, and heaven with Jesus that we can forget he confronted numerous instances of human sin. Because Christ's life and surroundings were rich in human experience, we should not be surprised that sinfulness is part of the mix. Jesus came to redeem us from sin, hence one can expect to find him encountering the sin from which he came to liberate us.

At the beginning of this seventeenth chapter, Jesus says that sin will inevitably occur, but those who tempt others to sin should have a stone tied around their necks and thrown into the sea. Such blunt words remind us that Jesus was not a sentimentalist about sin. He was well aware of evil and the temptation that leads to it.

The temptation process includes seven stages:

1. *Invitation.* Someone solicits us to do what is wrong. The act promises pleasure and is presented in an appealing manner. We are persuaded that the deed is somehow good, whether that be real or imagined. We do not think of ourselves as choosing evil directly. We open ourselves to what seems to be good and use our minds to lay aside what is evil in our choice.

2. *Feelings.* As the temptation takes hold of us, we let our feelings determine the morality of the act. The impact of the suggestion to evil is now felt in our emotions. Once our minds welcome the invitation to sin, our feelings — and even our bodies — respond. As the physical and emotional response grows, this causes us to experience inner conflict. Our minds may tell us that the deed is evil, but our feelings speak otherwise. It cannot be bad because it feels so

good. Feeling strives to be the source of judgement instead of intel-ligence. Our power to decide is now torn between mixed signals — our mind's moral principles and our feelings' enchantment with the anticipated pleasure.

3. *Decision.* We reach the moment of truth. If our conscience is strong, we will reject the temptation. If it wavers and capitulates to the pull of our passions and feelings, then our minds will rationalize the act. Then we decide to sin. That choice begins in our hearts before it becomes concrete behavior. Sin is first an evil inner choice and only then becomes a visible reality. That is why Jesus taught in his Sermon on the Mount that lust in the heart is already a sin even before any external act occurs, or that malice in the heart is already a sin before a vicious or murderous act takes place. Evil decisions first poison the heart and then the external performance. This is why we should develop an awareness of our inner life and its dramas so we can focus on the origin of evil there before it ever gets to visible be-havior.

4. *The Deed.* Eventually the internal sin assumes a visible form and becomes an evil action. Inner pride humiliates others. Inner lust will go on to rape and debase vulnerable people. Inner anger will proceed to beat and murder the innocent. Inner gluttony will ravage one's own body and deaden sensitivity to the hungry. Inner sloth will abet moral indifference to human need. Inner jealousy will break up marriages and poison friendships. The sin inside becomes the sin out-side. Temptation has found fulfillment.

5. *A Habit.* Temptation is never satisfied with one victory. Having weakened our minds with rationalizations and raised our feel-ings to preeminence in our judging procedures, temptation returns again to urge us to greater experiments with sinning. Temptation al-lures us into a moral desert where repeated acts of sin become a routine. We acquire the habit of attitudinal and behavioral evil. Gradually the dream of innocence fades and we assume that a life of evil is normal for us. We are then corrupted at the core, though the possibility of repentance and conversion is always available to us while we live.

6. *Captivity.* So deeply has temptation led us into a moral wilder-ness that we seem driven to sin rather than to act virtuously. Here our

behavior is akin to an immoral addiction. In biblical terms, this is the Babylonian captivity of the soul. Our hearts feel hardened in evil. Here more than ever we need a savior to liberate us. We are not inevitably determined to sin, but we feel so trapped in it that we wonder if salvation is possible.

7. *Hell.* If temptation's victories endure until our last breath then we have chosen to seal our compact with evil forever. After our death we will join the community of the damned. Having made evil a way of life on earth, we will take that inheritance with us into the next life. Having rejected saving love on earth, we will enter a realm of eternal non-love, the most acute form of pain possible for a human being whose fulfillment can only be satisfied by love. The triumphant smile of temptation will gaze on the bitterness of our faces.

This description of the seven stages of temptation does not take into account the complexity of human choices. It does not advert to the exceptions, circumstances, cultural factors, age variables, physical and mental weaknesses, family and social pressures that affect decision making. Granting all this, the reality of temptation, sin, and its consequences remain. We also never forget that forgiveness, mercy, love, and divine compassion are ever present as well. Liberation is as close as a heartbeat. Jesus himself followed his brief words about temptation with a reminder about the pervasive presence of divine forgiveness and the need for its reflection in human forgiving of others.

Upon hearing Christ's teaching about temptation and forgiveness, they properly realize they need an increase of spiritual faith if they are to live up to such ideals. The following story about faith puts us in touch with their hopes. Picture a cliff at the edge of a canyon. An iron pole at its edge holds onto one side of a strong wire that extends across the abyss to a similar holding point on the opposite cliff.

As you stand there looking at this, a man comes walking across the wire pushing a wheelbarrow with a person sitting in the vehicle. He successfully executes the frightening ride across the high wire and is now on your side of the canyon. You congratulate him on his achievement. He says to you, "Do you think I can do this again?" You might say yes, figuring he is an expert and could do it. But then he says to you, "All right, get in and I will take you across!" If you agree, your decision will be very much like what an act of faith in Christ is like.

You may feel your faith is very small. Jesus noted the same in his apostles. He recognized that their faith was as tiny as that of a mustard seed. That did not bother him. Nor should it deter us. Even the giant redwood trees in northern California began with a little seed. Yet from so unpromising a beginning there emerged trees so large that they could provide wood for hundreds of homes. All great things begin small. It is the potential of the faith that counts. Just as the seed of temptation can lead to the gross evil, so the seed of faith can lead to Christian nobility, character, and the heights of human wholeness.

Luke concludes this section of sayings with one of his numerous references to a meal as an image of life in the kingdom. Once again the reference is to the Christian attitude of loving service to one another.

What Were the Excuses of the Nine Lepers? (Lk. 17:11-19)

Jesus continued his journey to Jerusalem when he met ten lepers. They asked him for compassion. Jesus told them to go and show themselves to the priests. On the way, they found they were healed of their leprosy. Only one of them, a Samaritan, returned to thank him for the cure. Jesus asked where the other nine were.

Martin Bell, in his book, "The Way of the Wolf," offers an imaginative answer to Christ's question. He guesses that these might be the excuses they would have offered. The first one was simply too scared. He had always been a bashful person. He was grateful enough, but his disease had made him even more of a fearing person than ever. He was too frightened to come back and thank Jesus.

The second one did not like the idea of being cured so easily. He was of the opinion that one should earn healing. Why hadn't Jesus asked him to fast, practice a long list of challenging self denials, and say an extended list of prayers? He did not want a spiritual handout. He rejected what he perceived to be paternalism.

The third one realized that he liked the pain and humiliation of being a leper. He could not live without his problem. Yes, he might complain and make a fuss, but he enjoyed wallowing in his misery. Jesus had taken away his security blanket, miserable though it was.

The fourth one was simply so happy about what happened that he forgot to come back and say thanks. He was always known as a light headed and naive guy. So his ecstasy swept him away and he stumbled home without expressing gratitude.

The fifth one had been patronized so often by people that he could not bear to say thank you. He had endured do-gooders, working off their own guilt on the deprived so often, that he despised them. He hated the look in their eyes that asked for appreciation. They were more interested in feeling good themselves than in helping him. He was not a scrooge by nature, but such treatment had hardened him. He was wrong about Jesus, but too blind to see it.

The sixth one was a wife and a mother. For years she dreamed about reunion with her family. Night after night she visualized how she would hug her husband and love her children. She was not ungrateful to Jesus. But her homing instinct and her bottomless craving for her family pushed her to rush home.

The seventh one was an agnostic. He simply did not believe in miracles. To him the cure was merely a case of spontaneous remission. He went through the rituals of appearing before the clergy simply to be civil. An enlightened man by his own estimation, he rejected both superstitious magic and religious miracle. Somehow his cure was explainable. There was no need to thank Jesus.

It was the eighth leper's faith that prevented him from thanking Jesus. He knew Christ had cured him. He felt his gratitude would be best expressed by going out and telling other people the good news about Jesus. There was no time to delay the announcement of the kingdom.

The excuse of the ninth leper remains a puzzle. No one will ever know. He gave no clues. He looked pleased enough. He felt his body carefully for leprous lumps. He checked his face in the pond's reflection. He muttered a bit and drifted away. Sometimes you just will never know a person's reasons.

This interpretation of the story reminds us to be cautious in our judgement of others' behavior. It does not mean that gratitude should not be shown. The responsibility is with the beneficiary. The giver must not force the thanks.

"When the giver insists that thanks be said
The gold in the gift turns to lead."

Jesus knew whatever were the excuses of the nine lepers. When he asks the question, "Where are the other nine?" look at the smile in his eyes.

Advance Notice of Christ's Second Coming (Lk. 17:20-37)

These passages about the coming of the kingdom of God and the coming of the Son of Man need some distinctions. The Pharisees ask how they could tell the kingdom of God was coming. Jesus answers that it has already come and is not accompanied by extraordinary signs like those that will announce the second coming. Jesus is himself the greatest sign of the arrival of God's kingdom. His teachings and miracles are the visible evidence of its arrival.

To his disciples Jesus talks about the signs of the second coming. It is an experience that they will long for when they face the problems of Gospel ministry after he is gone. It is not something that will be easily discerned. It will come to everyone as a surprise, much like the flash of lightning that comes suddenly and from an unexpected direction.

It will have the quality of earlier judgement events such as the flood that came in the days of Noah and the fire that consumed the city of Sodom in the days of Lot and his wife. Noah and the saved entered the ark, while the others who failed to live by spiritual values will perish. Lot's wife dallied to see the destruction of her home and lost her chance for salvation by looking back instead of to her saving future.

Jesus told them they will need the faith of Noah and the steadfastness of Lot. Worrying about saving earthly life and possessions, as was the case of Lot's wife, will not be the best approach to the second coming. People who try to save their lives will lose them. Those who let their old lives be lost will gain their real lives in Christ. This is another form of Luke's memory of Christ's basic teaching: Lose the self. Take the cross. Follow Jesus.

When that fateful day does come, human relationships and friendships and acquaintances will not be the issue. Some will be taken and others will be left. Intimacy with a good person is not a guarantee of one's own salvation. Each person faces the judgement according to the way that person has loved, forgiven, and accepted the rules of Christ's discipleship. We cannot let someone else fulfill our personal responsibilities.

Jesus will return again to this theme of judgement just before the beginning of his passion (Lk. 21).

Reflection

1. How would I describe the process of temptation?
2. What makes the temptation to sin positive and appealing?
3. What is wrong with the statement, "It can't be bad because it feels so good?"
4. How can I tell that sin happens inside before it occurs outside?
5. Why is temptation never satisfied with one victory?
6. When seemingly trapped in an immoral captivity what should one do?
7. Why is hell the logical outcome of a soul sealed in sin?
8. How can I balance this description of the seven stages of temptation with my awareness of all the factors that affect moral decision making?
9. What is my reaction to the imagined excuses of the nine lepers?
10. How do I react when I am not thanked for a favor done or an act of love offered to another?

Prayer

Lord Jesus, you have known some of the earlier stages of temptation. Since you never sinned, you did not experience all seven stages. Deliver me from temptation and its many stages. Fill me with perceptive faith to recognize the presence and power of temptation. Rescue me from rationalizing away my sinfulness. Save me now and move me to be grateful for your redemptive acts.

18 Pray with Persistence, Humility, and Simplicity

Jesus Teaches Three Lessons on Prayer (Lk. 18:1-17)

In Tennyson's poem, "Morte d'Arthur," the final scene describes Arthur saying good-bye to his faithful servant and long time friend. Arthur's final words are about prayer. "And you, that look upon my face, pray for my soul. For more things are wrought by prayer than this world dreams of. For a man is no better than a sheep or a goat that nourishes the blind life within the brain, if he lift not his heart in prayer."

We have noted that Luke emphasizes Christ's teachings on prayer. In this eighteenth chapter Luke recalls three lessons from Jesus on the attitudes one should have in prayer. They are (1) Persistence, (2) Humility, (3) Simplicity.

Persistence. Jesus told a story about a widow who persisted in persuading a resistant judge — who neither feared God nor was intimidated by any person — to award her justice in her court case. The tough judge yielded to the widow both because she "bothered" him so much and he, fearless though he was, worried she would hit him. The humorous picture of a "Miss Marple-like widow" assaulting a stern judge was just the right touch in communicating the need to be resolute and persistent in prayer.

It is not uncommon for people to wonder how long they should keep praying for their intentions. The pilgrimage of prayer seems to weary and discourage them. The journey image is helpful. In taking a trip we start out with enthusiasm and feel liberated as we leave our customary world behind. As the days of the trip pass by, we become fatigued. We encounter the numerous irritations that are part of any voyage — delays, cold food, lost luggage, bad weather, tedious fellow travelers, lumpy beds, colds, wrong turns, dwindling cash, and too many stairs.

Exasperated travelers often stop and say, "Is this worth it?

Should I go on with it?" Seasoned travelers will reply that the journey is worth it despite the annoyances. They remind us that we must not think too much of how we feel. Sensibly, they note that self absorption is the best way to miss the bus. When we think too much about ourselves, we miss our connections.

The same is true in prayer. Persistence means forging ahead despite the distractions of the journey. We must not grow weary or spend energy worrying about how well we are doing in beseeching God for whatever is our intention. The crisp old lady of Christ's story is a model for us. The frustrating judge did not deter her. She did not waste time licking her wounds or nursing self pity. Onward and upward was her motto. That should be ours, too.

Humility. Great people are usually humble folks. When the famous Adlai Stevenson lost the election to Eisenhower, he was invited by President Truman to spend the night in the Lincoln Room at the White House. When Stevenson was undressed and ready to retire, he hesitated in awe before the bed. He could not dream of sleeping in so important a bed, so he slept on the sofa. What that great and humble man did not know was that in Lincoln's day that bed was not there. But the sofa was.

The celebrated Jimmy Durante had a soft spot in his heart for the frailties of people. He once said, "There are more good people in the world than bad ones. I don't mind if a man strikes a match on the furniture so long as he goes with the grain."

Winston Churchill once attended a banquet in the Savoy Hotel in London. The great and famous filled the tables. For the evening's entertainment the celebrities were asked, "If you couldn't be who you are, who would you like to be?" Churchill rose and said, "If I could not be who I am, then I would like to be" — and then the 78-year-old Sir Winston turned to touch his wife's hand — "Lady Churchill's second husband."

Jesus held that humility is an essential characteristic of prayer. Snobs are not going to pray very well. Self-inflated people may never truly understand how to pray so long as they remain puffed up. His story about the prayer of a self-important Pharisee and a humble tax collector made this point. The law said the official religious leaders should give the temple one-tenth of their income. It only required a fast once a year on the Day of Atonement.

The Pharisee of the story fasted on Monday's and Thursday's, market days when crowds would notice him, face whitened and clothes rumpled to signal the fast. He also tithed more than was demanded. In his prayer he informed God that he was not like sinners, but tithed and fasted even more than observant believers. He was not really praying, but instructing God about how good and devout he was. To him prayer was a matter of self advertisement. His attention was on himself and his so-called meritorious deeds, not on God. His religion was simply theater where he won his own "Oscar" for the best performance at the temple.

The despised and humble tax collector stood in the shadows in a corner of the temple where no one would see him but God. He also talked about himself to God, but he only wanted to confess his sins and shortcomings to the Lord, not display his religious achievements. He beat his breast and quietly prayed over and over, "O God, be merciful to me a sinner" (verse 13). Jesus praised the humble tax man for his humility. The one who prays humbly will be exalted. The one who exalts himself will be humbled.

The man who was officially great had too much pride to admit his sinfulness. The man who was officially detestable had enough humility to confess his sins. Pride robbed the Pharisee of self insight. Humility revealed to the tax collector the truth of his situation. The Pharisee prayed to himself. The tax collector prayed to God. Humility is the gift of this parable.

Simplicity. People were fond of bringing their children to Jesus so he could bless them. Luke says the apostles tried to stop this. Apparently they felt that the noisy, exuberant children interrupted the more important "adult" religious gathering. Salvation was too serious a business to be diverted by playfulness with kids. Perhaps children should be seen, but not heard and certainly not hugged, touched, and loved by Jesus. Our Lord loved to have children around him and did not agree at all with his apostles on this matter.

Often Jesus would hold up a child, as in this case, and remind everyone that the simplicity of a child teaches everyone the kind of attitude one needs in order to enter the kingdom of heaven. "Whoever does not accept the kingdom of God like a child will not enter it" (verse 17).

This childlike simplicity is another characteristic of genuine prayer. The older we get, the more complex we become. We forget what it was like to see the world with simplicity. Conflicting demands hound us on all sides. Culture challenges us to be sophisticated. Scholars caution us to be nuanced. Opinion makers warn us about life's ambiguities. To be simple is to be simple-minded.

The web of the world chokes us with its never ending complex links. Facts drown us. Exceptions paralyze our decision making strength. The lost innocence of our childhood may seem like a cruel joke. We think we shall never again go home to childhood, except in the clinical second childhood and senility of old age. But Jesus urges us to become childlike again, not children, but youthful with the simplicity that sees the world in terms of unity rather than complexity. The world has a unity as well as a diversity. Prayerful simplicity contemplates the unity.

The Spiritual Danger of Wealth (Lk. 18:18-30)

The prosperous members of today's affluent societies should listen intently to Christ's words to the wealthy. A rich man asked him what he should do to inherit eternal life. Listing the major commandments, Jesus pointed out these were roads to heaven. The man said he had kept these commandments faithfully all his life. Even he sensed they were not enough. Jesus realized the rich man was basically open to a deeper challenge, so he told him to let go of all his wealth, give it to the poor, and follow him. It was too great a demand for him. With a sad face he walked away.

Jesus was also sad about this and remarked how hard it is for people with great possessions to commit themselves to the kingdom, harder than for a camel to squeeze through the eye of a needle. His listeners believed that prosperity was a sign of God's favor, hence they wondered who could be saved if the apparently redeemed were not so after all. Jesus reminded them that in God's plans this could be done. Peter spoke up flaunting the fact they had left all their possessions to follow him. What would they get for it? He heard the Lord tell him that they would be rewarded with far more than they surrendered.

Years later, Timothy, a disciple of Peter would echo the words of Jesus just as bluntly. "We brought nothing into the world, just as we shall not be able to take anything out of it. If we have food and clothing, we should be content with that. Those who want to be rich are falling into temptation and into a trap and into many foolish and harmful desires, which plunge them into ruin and destruction. For the love of money is the root of all evil" (I Tim. 6:9-10).

It is a well known fact that wealth does not guarantee happiness. Hundreds of stories of unhappy and unfulfilled rich people have been told often enough. Depression, addiction, suicide, betrayal, murder, and other ills frequently enough afflict the prosperous.

More to the point here is Christ's observation that wealth endangers the eternal interests of people. The time it takes to acquire and take care of money uses up energy that might be devoted to faith and charity. The love of money distracts the mind from God and deadens the attention to faith filled motivation. Worldly engagements excite us and consume us. The more we set our hearts on them, the more we withdraw from God.

Scripture has many examples of the negative effect of possessions on the rich. David's story is a notable case of the corrupting influence of affluence. He seemed a lot happier as a simple shepherd than when he became the king of Israel. With composure, the young shepherd advanced on Goliath with trust in God. He thought to himself that the God who delivered him from the claws of the lion would preserve him from the hand of the Philistine giant.

Compare that with the state of his life after he ascended the throne with all its gold, glory, and possessions. There he collected a bowl full of troubles and demonstrated shameful weaknesses and inconsistencies. He seduced Bathsheba and caused the judicial murder of her husband Uriah at the battlefront so he could make her his wife. His son Absalom became estranged from him. True, God's grace finally prevailed in his life and David died in peace with the Lord. Power and wealth almost killed his soul, an experience which would seem less likely had he remained a shepherd.

His son Solomon, the very epitome of scriptural wealth and grandeur, is a far sadder instance of the corruption of riches. Scripture does not say he repented in the end, so we do not know if God's grace finally prevailed in his life. Instead Scripture says this hugely wealthy man indulged himself with many strange women. In his old age, they turned his heart away from God. The old king knelt before fertility gods.

This was the man who composed a glorious prayer for the dedication of the temple. God was so pleased with him then that he asked him what his heart most desired. Solomon replied that he wanted nothing less than an understanding heart — far preferable to a long life and riches. What happened to him along life's journey? The seduction of riches turned his heart and he rejected the very gift of wisdom offered to him.

The possession of the goods of this world presents unique dangers to those who have them. That is why Scripture says that God purifies those whom he loves. St. Paul was not rich, but he did possess abundant spiritual talents. He could preach like an angel, write like a poet, and work like a horse. Yet even spiritual riches could have spoiled him and tainted his soul. So much in need was he of purification that even his sufferings, anxieties, and prodigious exertions were not enough to keep him in line. Beyond this God gave him a thorn in the flesh to keep him humble and prevent him from a poisonous form of pride, self-satisfaction in his spiritual wealth.

What then shall guide the wealthy Christian? Certainly, restraint from being absorbed by the world made so easily available by wealth. Second, a heart full of thanks for the good that is contained in the fruits of the earth and the products of effort. Third, a hunger to give glory to God by means of our possessions. Fourth, an ever deepening spirit of generosity at the personal and social level. Last, the cautious attitude that stops us from ever thinking that acquisitiveness will make us happier.

Jesus Heals a Blind Beggar (Lk. 18:35-43)

Christ's attention to a rich man now changes to a poor one, a blind beggar. At the gates of Jericho he met a blind beggar who shouted to him for mercy. Some people tried to quiet the man who thereupon yelled all the louder for pity. Jesus heard him and asked what he wanted. The man begged him for the gift of sight. Jesus immediately said, "Have sight. Your faith has saved you" (verse 42).

The story reinforces Christ's teaching about persistence in prayer and the fact that prayers are answered. The man glorified God and the people echoed his praise. Lastly, Jesus could heal the poor man because he was open to faith. He could not help the rich one because that man was closed to the offer of Christ.

Reflection

1. How persistent have I been in praying?
2. How have I thought that my religious practices have entitled me to receive God's blessings?
3. What stories can I tell about people whose prayer reflects their humble attitude in life?
4. What means do I use to get beyond the complexities of life so I can develop a childlike attitude of simplicity of heart?
5. I know that sinners are found among the rich and poor alike. How does wealth open a person to sinfulness?
6. If David had remained a shepherd, how might he have avoided the sinfulness that afflicted him when he became a king?
7. How could Solomon who prayed for wisdom more than riches have turned out to be an idolater?
8. If I had been talking to the rich young man of the gospel what would I have said?
9. What do I think of Timothy's statement that love of money is the root of all evil?
10. What lesson do I learn from the cure of the blind beggar?

Prayer

Jesus, model of prayer, you constantly went aside, sometimes all night, in order to pray. You were persistent, humble, and simple in your approach to praying. You taught these values in your sermons. Fill me with the grace of prayer and the attitudes that make prayer effective. Turn my heart always to you.

19   Some Good News for the Rich

A Rich Man Can Be Saved (Lk. 19:1-10)

The story of the conversion of Zaccheus proves that a rich man can be saved. Contrast his experience with that of the rich man in Luke 18:18-30.

The conversion of Zaccheus occurred in Jericho. Archaeologists have found traces of village life at Jericho dating back over 10,000 years, making it one of the oldest known, continuously inhabited cities in the world. Called the "City of Palms," Jericho was the Palm Springs resort of its day, warm and sunny enough to attract the wealthy and their estates. Herod the Great built a palace there and used it as his winter capital.

Jericho is fourteen miles from Jerusalem. Their climates radically differ. Situated 2,500 feet up in the highlands, Jerusalem has damp and chilly winters. Exactly the opposite, Jericho rests in so deep a valley — 840 feet below sea level — that its winters are warm. An extensive oasis surrounded Jericho. A well developed irrigation system was the source of the luxuriant greenery that bordered the city. Balm was one of Jericho's prime exports.

Jesus had many associations with Jericho. The traditional site of his Jordan baptism was five miles east of the city. The traditional locale for his temptations in the desert is the "Mountain of the Temptation," several miles northwest of Jericho. His parable of the Good Samaritan takes place in a narrow pass that leads from Jericho to Jerusalem.

It is not surprising, therefore, that Jesus would have found a rich man in a community that was a haven for the wealthy. It was also a gold mine for tax collectors — and probably for tax evaders. Walking through the city, Jesus attracted a large crowd. The tax collector, Zaccheus, wanted to see Jesus, but he was a short man (verse 3) and was unable to catch a glimpse of the Lord. Little Zaccheus emerges from the gospel page as a charming and loveable figure. He is the scrappy little fellow who climbs a sycamore tree to see Jesus.

As a tax collector, Zaccheus was not liked, both because he collaborated with the Romans and often cheated the people from whom
he collected the taxes. Yet, there was a basic goodness in this man.
He did not simply want to see Jesus out of curiosity. He felt a yearning for Jesus. He did not search for a celebrity but a savior. He was
probably pushy and ambitious, but his character was made of sterner
stuff as soon became clear. While the adoring crowds craved attention from Jesus, little Zaccheus gazed humbly on him from a branch
of a sycamore tree.

Jesus looked beyond all the celebrity seekers and chose a humble
man for his love and friendship. Jesus went against the popular tide
of local prejudice. He found a good man and wanted everyone to
know about it. He looked up at the rapt little man and urged him to
come down. "Today I must stay at your house" (verse 5). What a
lovely experience for a man, socially isolated at the bottom of
society, to be singled out for this honor.

Usually we are the ones who hope we can be spiritual enough to
say, "I must be with Jesus." Here it is Christ who speaks the language of
"must." Jesus wants an intimate form of relating to Zaccheus, not just as
a teacher with a student in a public square, but as a friend who will sit at
table in the sanctuary of this delighted man's home.

The crowd grumbled that Jesus would socialize with a sinner.
The outspoken Zaccheus was thrilled and said out loud in front of
them all that he would give half of his possessions to the poor.
Moreover, he will repay anyone he cheated four times over. Jesus
matched the generosity of this rich man and told the world that our
little friend had received salvation. Here at last is a rich "camel" that
did squeeze through the eye of the needle.

Ten Gold Coins —
Investment Advice from Jesus (Lk. 19:11-27)

Now a discussion arose about the near arrival of the kingdom as
they approached Jerusalem. They still had the political, not the spiritual
view, of Christ's kingdom. Jesus told a parable directed at those who
would be the shepherds of his spiritual kingdom, the church.

A nobleman made plans for a trip to receive the kingship of a certain country. Before leaving he called his servants and gave each of them ten gold coins. He instructed them to trade with these coins until he came back. When he returned from his trip, he interviewed each servant and listened to the results of their investments. The first one said he had gained ten new coins. The master praised him and gave him charge of ten cities. The second one gained five coins and was rewarded with five cities. The last servant came, fearfully clutching the five coins he had received in a protective handkerchief. He said he was so afraid of his master that he feared to invest the money. At least he could give back what he received. The master showed his anger at this timid servant and told him he was foolish to have done nothing. At least he could have put the money in the bank where it could obtain interest. He ordered the money to be taken from this servant and given to the others. The moral of the story: Those to whom much has been given — and who make it multiply — more will be added. Those who do nothing with their gifts, the little they have will be taken away. Use it or lose it.

In this instance Jesus decided not to confront directly their false understandings of his kingdom. Instead he took an example from the way political kingdoms are run and applied it to those who would be the spiritual shepherds of the kingdom of God. The fearful, timid shepherd who hoards the gifts of the Gospel truths and the sacraments, not feeding people with this life giving bread, will be repudiated by Christ for leaving the people as sheep without a shepherd. The shepherd who refuses to minister energetically will be rejected.

Palm Sunday (Lk. 19:28-48)

Passover week began. Each family selected a passover lamb. In the procession of the palms on Sunday, the people would unwittingly select Jesus as their Passover Lamb. They waved the palm branches of choice on Sunday and by Friday the thorns at the roots of the palms would be plaited as a crown for his head.

The evening before, Jesus relaxed at Bethany with his dearest friends, Martha, Mary, and Lazarus. But there was some business to take care of. He instructed two of his disciples to go to a certain house in the village and bring him a colt. They were to tell the owner that Jesus had need of it.

As one who owned nothing, Jesus was an inveterate borrower. He borrowed Peter's boat as a sea-borne pulpit. He borrowed the loaves and fishes from a boy to feed the 5,000. He borrowed a grave that would be the scene of his resurrection. The last week of his life began with borrowing a colt for his entrance into Jerusalem.

Bethany is on the east slope of the Mount of Olives. From there to Jerusalem is about a two-mile walk. On Sunday the disciples threw their cloaks on the colt. Jesus mounted it and set out for the Holy City. News of his coming had spread. A crowd came out to greet him. They spread their cloaks on the road — like a red carpet to greet a king.

Never before had Jesus willingly let himself be the center of attention for an adoring multitude. Consistently, he had deflected attention from himself, urging people to think of his teachings, reform their lives, and begin a life of love and forgiveness. He asked people not to spread word about his miracles — especially astounding ones like the raising of the daughter of Jairus. He did not want to arouse the mass religious hysteria that such cures would engender.

When he granted Peter, James, and John an intimate glimpse of his inner glory, he strictly forbade them to speak about it to anyone. People must come to him in the darkness of the mystery of faith, not blinded and mesmerized by a glory that gave them no chance to make a personal decision. At the miracle of the loaves the people wanted to make him a political king. Jesus fled from their aspirations. He would not be the pawn of an enthusiastic rebellion. Only peaceful faith would attain him, not class warfare.

Now, for the first time, Jesus allowed himself to be the hero of an admiring throng, the center of popular acclaim. Why did he change his position, so strongly held in all other situations? One thing is clear. He certainly did not seek the praise of the people. He had no interest in popularity. He did not yearn for a high rating in the local polls. He was not a politician charming his constituency. He was a savior seeking to challenge people to accept him in faith.

This was his last historic chance to offer people the option for love, the option for him as their savior. They praised him as king when they sang their hosannas. He would again disabuse them of their mistaken notion of his kingship. Nonetheless, he selected the royal city of the Passover as the site to make his last appeal to all of them to see who he really was and accept the salvation he offered them.

He was indeed a king, but a king of hearts, not a ruler of nations. He allowed himself to enter Jerusalem precisely as a spiritual king, clothed with the imagery of the prophet Zechariah.

Rejoice heartily, O daughter of Zion,
shout for joy, O daughter Jerusalem!
See your king shall come to you;
a just savior is he,
Meek, and riding on an ass,
on a colt, the foal of an ass.

—Zec. 9:9

Zechariah noted that the king in his imagery is a savior. He has the majesty of love and grace, but also a meekness and humility to offset any vanity or pomp. Surviving carvings of ancient kings proceeding in triumph show men who marched in pride, sometimes walking over (or even riding over) the bodies of their enemies. They made their parades a show of strength, a manifestation of power designed to dominate the viewers and send pangs of fear into their bones.

Jesus stressed the meekness, not the power. He emphasized the humility, not the ruthlessness. The Roman soldiers who gazed on this ragged procession of local provincials quickly judged they had little to fear. As Pilate stared from his Fortress Antonia, he smiled with relief. That foolish figure on an ass would not give him much trouble this busy week.

All these witnesses, of course, were wrong. The multitude of admirers thought they had a new David on their hands. He seemed to nurse their dreams of former glory. The Romans judged they were dealing with a harmless holy man, one who would probably pacify the people in a week when things could get out of hand. Accustomed to battle and the small skirmishes their policing brought about, they sized Jesus up as a non-fighter. This non-violent man would actually be a benefit to them, a silent accomplice in their never ending task of keeping the peace. Had he looked a little more pleased with the flattery, they might have been more cautious. No, this Jesus would cause them no trouble.

Only the religious leaders disliked what they saw. Not that they understood the true meaning of Christ's mission, but all along they correctly judged that Jesus was a threat to their perception of the role and destiny of religion in the lives of their people. They were wrong about him also, but for a different reason. In their vision, he undermined their authority and would be a source of popular discontent. As they listened to the acclamations of the assembly, they were profoundly disturbed and sought to stem this new level of the people's devotion to Jesus.

"Teacher, rebuke your disciples."

"I tell you that if they keep silence, the stones will cry out!" (verses 39-40).

Were the people to be silent, mother nature herself would cry out her praise to the Lord of creation.

Jesus was now near to entering Jerusalem. From the vantage point of height on the Mount of Olives, he could see her beauty and her glory. He knew it would also be the scene of his suffering and death. It symbolized the best and the worst in humanity.

Jesus loved Jerusalem. As a young boy of twelve he had sung the pilgrim's praise of the city. "I rejoiced because they said to me, 'We will go up to the house of the Lord.' And now we have set foot within your gates, O Jerusalem" (Ps. 122:1-2). In his heart echoed the words of Isaiah, "Speak tenderly to Jerusalem" (Is. 40:1). "I create Jerusalem to be a joy and its people to be a delight" (Is. 65:18).

In the midst of the hosannas, Jesus began to cry. Self pity about his days ahead did not move him. Sorrow about the future of the city of the covenant distressed him. He foresaw the tragedy that would destroy all this beauty and cause untold suffering to his beloved people.

The celebrants in the parade grew silent as they heard him say, "They will smash you to the ground and your children within you" (verse 44). The words of Jeremiah lingered in his heart. "Gone from Zion is all her glory. . . . At this I weep, my eyes run with tears" (Lam. 1:6,16). His tears and words momentarily stilled and puzzled the festive crowd. They did not want to lose their happy feelings and they had no wisdom to see what Jesus meant. Determined to carry the joyful mood of the day, they resumed their praises and led Jesus in triumph through the gates of Jerusalem.

Jesus completed his Palm Sunday march by entering the temple. He proceeded to cleanse it of the money changers and those who cheated the people by selling sacrificial animals at unfair prices. He condemned such commercialism as totally unsuited to a house of prayer and the home of God.

The paschal journey of Jesus was reaching its final phase. Luke noted that when the Galilean ministry was finished, Jesus would never veer from his destiny. "When the days for his being taken up were fulfilled, he resolutely determined to journey to Jerusalem" (Lk. 9:51). At last he has walked into Jerusalem, the eye of the storm. His bold act in the temple revealed that he was not a sentimental dreamer about holiness and justice, but a doer of the will of God.

Reflection

1. Why was Jericho a setting where Jesus was likely to meet a tax collector?
2. What are the attractive qualities of Zaccheus that drew Jesus to engage him?
3. How did Zaccheus plan to reimburse those whom he had cheated?
4. How would I feel if Jesus said to me that he felt he must come into my heart?
5. God has given me my version of the "ten coins" of the parable. How have I invested these gifts from God?
6. What lesson do I learn from the "borrowings" (the boat, the bread, the colt) of Jesus?
7. How might I have misunderstood the real meaning of Christ's Palm Sunday entry to Jerusalem?
8. How do Christ's tears over Jerusalem affect me?
9. What kind of a cleansing of my "temple" do I need from Jesus?
10. What lessons about discipleship do I learn in this chapter?

Prayer

Resolute Jesus, from the time you completed your Galilean ministry you never were distracted from your resolve to go to Jerusalem and there enter into the paschal mystery which saved me. Fill my heart with this kind of faith determination so that my witness to love and forgiveness may never falter. Let my heart's resolve be such that my mind will always follow its goals of faith.

20 The Power of Personal Authority

Personal and Institutional Authority (Lk. 20:1-8)

In his first two actions in Passover Week, Jesus behaved as a man with authority. At the Palm Sunday procession he robed himself in the authoritative imagery of Zechariah's Savior King. In cleansing the temple, Jesus asserted his moral authority in purifying the House of God from the desecration of greedy merchants. He aggressively revealed his spiritual and moral authority. Yet he had no institutional support for this. He was not an official member of the priestly order which claimed spiritual authority over the people. He was not an accredited member of the community of the Scribes and Pharisees who occupied the chairs of moral authority. He was not even old enough to be an "elder."

Jesus possessed none of the accepted symbols of public authority. Yet he acted with an authority that eclipsed those who boasted of their institutional support. His personal authority outshone those who made loud noises about their authoritative importance. Jesus let his integrity speak for itself. His adversaries were so unsure of their authority that they insisted on speaking from the vantage points of their positions in society. They felt secure when they could verify their importance either from membership in a priestly family or from a proven record of study in one or another rabbinical school. Jesus preached what he practiced. They preached what they inherited or studied.

The people could tell the difference between personal and institutional authority. This is why the priests and scribes approached him while he was teaching the Good News in the temple and asked him, "Tell us, by what authority are you doing these things? Or who is the one who gave you this authority?" (verse 2). Jesus responded with the "Irish answer," that is, he asked them a question in turn. He asked them whether John's baptism was from heavenly or human origin.

They had intended to embarrass him in front of his rapt pupils. They knew he had no publicly acceptable authority to act like a Savior King or to take moral charge of the temple's marketplace. They were desperate to undermine the enthusiastic respect he was receiving. They wanted to assail his credibility. They were not sincere searchers for the truth. They were ecclesiastical rascals trying to eliminate a troublesome rival. They already savored the pleasure of his presumed discomfort.

Jesus was ready for their lame attempt to discredit him. He presented them with a dilemma far more damaging to them. Very likely he smiled as he watched them deservedly squirm. Any answer they tried to give would shame them in front of the people — and in the temple of all places.

If they said the Baptist acted from a heavenly mandate, they would then have to explain why they did not support him. Since they claimed they were in possession of interpreting the divine manifestations in human life, why did they fail to see it in the Baptist's life and ministry? Why did they refuse to believe in him? If they said the Baptist simply operated from a purely human impulse, they would anger the people. That judgement would be so dangerous, they would find the people picking up stones to pummel them. So they just stood there in frustrated and furious silence. At last one of them weakly said that they did not know where the Baptist's position on baptism came from.

Possibly Jesus gave an innocent shrug at that point. If they could not answer so simple a question, how could he proceed to offer them a response weighted with the mystery of divinity. Why offer them a reply that needed faith to appreciate it, when they did not even have enough belief to recognize God's action in the Baptist? "Neither shall I tell you by what authority I do these things" (verse 8).

The point at issue here is faith, not the various sources of authority. Jesus had great respect for both personal and institutional authority. His authority visibly seemed to be purely personal in human and cultural terms. In fact, from the perspective of faith, his authority was from God. The official representatives of God, lacking faith in him, reduced the question of authority to a matter of institutional certification. They did not discern the Spirit working in him, so they failed to realize who he really was and what was the source of his compelling witness.

They Killed the Landlord's Son (Lk. 20:9-19)

Up to this point the mood was playful, a slightly humorous exchange of wits, a typical battle between people accustomed to the small victories of religious debate. Not too much seemed to be at stake so long as the participants had room to maneuver. But Jesus had not come to Jerusalem for another bout of rabbinic banter. This was the last stage in his paschal journey. The serious business of his death was at hand.

He told a story that chilled the happy feelings of his Palm Sunday admirers and confirmed the growing awareness of his religious adversaries that they must get rid of this man. Jesus simply let them know this was exactly what they would inevitably do. His story was about people not paying their rent, a topic bound to catch everyone's interest.

Rich wine growers often had many vineyards spread far and wide. The only way they could cultivate all these sources of income was to hire tenant vintners to do the work for them, in return for a rental fee, which was usually a substantial portion of the harvested grapes. When the vineyards were far away from the control of the landlord, it was not uncommon for the tenants to default on their rent. They reasoned that the plenitude of grapes was due to their efforts, that the landlord was charging too much anyway, that they were safely out of harm's way, often in another country. So why not beat up the rent collectors and forget their contracts?

Jesus told this all too familiar story, but then added a fresh detail. The landlord's son came to get the rent. Jesus watched his listeners grow more attentive. The son would surely solve the problem. It would be like having the landlord himself arrive. As they awaited this predictable resolution, they were startled to hear Jesus say that the tenants decided to kill the son and take over the vineyards themselves. Murder followed by outright robbery.

Normally, the people had a secret liking for the tenants who made it hard for an owner to collect rent. Rich people had too much money anyhow. A little gentle rebellion never hurt anyone. But the fresh addition Jesus brought to the story shocked them. Marginal rebellion had become murder and theft.

"Let it not be so!" (verse 16). There is the universal voice of moral conscience. Spontaneously, people will yell out the moral truth when it really needs to be heard. Of course this should not be so. Jesus drew them to think about the real point of his story. He quoted Psalm 118:22 about the rejected stone which had become the cornerstone. In English the application does not make as much sense, until we are instructed that in Hebrew this would have been part of a pun, for the word for son is "ben" and the word for stone is "eben." The son of the story is himself. He will be rejected and killed. But his enemies will not triumph, for as the prophetic psalm verse says the rejected one will become the cornerstone of a new structure.

It is not clear whether the people appreciated Christ's interpretation. They did not yet think of him as endangered. But Luke tells us that the scribes and chief priests understood immediately what he meant. The story aroused their intentions to do exactly what the murderous tenants had done, so much so that they wanted to grab him then and there, except their fear of the people prevented them. Let it not be so!

Caesar's Coin (Lk. 20:20-26)

Luke follows up with another controversy story which builds the tension of Passover Week and logically leads to the tragedy ahead. The religious leaders wanted a pretext for arresting Jesus. They sent representatives, pretending to be devout believers, to trap him. They flattered Jesus by pronouncing his teachings as truth and praising his impartiality and moral courage in teaching the real way to God, exactly the opposite of their real opinions about him.

In front of witnesses whose aversion to taxes was a national pastime, they asked Jesus if it was all right to pay taxes to Caesar. Presumably, if Jesus said yes, he would lose the affection and loyalty of people who thought Roman taxes were a gross injustice. If he said no, then he could be reported to the Romans as a subversive on the tax issue.

Jesus asked for a coin. He knew they were not sincere in their question. He held up the coin and asked them whose image was on it. They told him that it was Caesar's. "Then repay to Caesar what belongs to Caesar and to God what belongs to God" (verse 25).

Jesus was not a tax rebel, nor was he interested in armed revolt to achieve justice. He certainly wanted peace and justice for his people, but his method of achieving it would be non-violent spirituality, not the point of a sword. His argument was that the desired change in the social, political, and economic order would occur when hearts and attitudes changed, not by external forms of violence. His teachings amazed the people and reduced the questioners to silence.

Which Man Is Her Real Husband? (Lk. 20:27-40)

The controversy stories continue with a challenge about the reality and meaning of resurrection. The Sadducees denied the reality of resurrection. Their question posed to Jesus was a cynical one meant to underline the silliness of believing in resurrection. They posed what was probably one of their typical absurd case studies designed to make belief in resurrection seem foolish.

They began with the Levirate law of Moses which taught that if a husband dies without issue, his brother may marry his wife in order that the male line would survive in offspring. Then came their application of the law to a woman whose husband had six brothers. The husband died leaving no children. Then one after another, the other six brothers married her and died before children were born. Which man would be her real husband at the resurrection?

Jesus knew just what they were getting at. He told them that because they do not believe in resurrection, their basic assumption prevented them from understanding the unique nature of resurrected life, which is not the same as earthly life. Here people marry. In resurrected life they do not.

He drove home the point more forcefully by showing them to be unsophisticated literalists when it came to the Hebrew Scriptures.

They did not believe in resurrection because they could not find a passage that says it happens. Jesus quoted a scriptural passage that has God saying — after the death of these patriarchs — that he is the God of Abraham, Isaac, and Jacob. They had to admit that God is the God of the living, not the dead, hence resurrected life must be possible to the patriarchs. Jesus impressed even some of the scribes who did believe in resurrection. "Teacher, you have answered well" (verse 39).

Closing Arguments (Lk. 20:41-47)

The next encounter was not a dialogue but a puzzler presented by Jesus to the religious scholars. In the dreams of all good Jews, the messiah would be the Son of David. The scribes taught as much. The blind man of Jericho addressed Jesus with this title and the crowds on Palm Sunday did the same. Now Jesus asked a question that appeared to dispute this well received teaching. He quoted the first verse of Psalm 110 where David said he heard God talk to the anointed one (the messiah) and ask him to sit at his right hand. David spoke of the messiah as "My Lord." Jesus asked the scribes, "If David calls him 'Lord,' how can he be his son?" (verse 43).

All we hear from Christ's listeners is a numbed silence. This was another instance of Christ's efforts to budge everyone from the mistaken notion that the messiah would be a new David, a dashing poet king, a romantic Jewish military hero who would bring back a long lost glory. Jesus was not denying that the messiah would be the son of David. He could hardly do so since he was in fact that son. But he was a much different person than the one conceived by popular mythology.

The messiah would not be a political-military king, but rather a spiritual leader establishing the kingdom of God, a religious figure rooting in this world the possibility of God's rule in each human heart. In retrospect this seems so obvious and true. But seen from the perspective of his hearers prior to the cross, the resurrection, and the sending of the Spirit, this was the most alien notion imaginable.

One would think that today the idea of a political Christ-messiah never would come up. Yet in some extreme forms of liberation theology, this is just the Christ being advocated. Just as the people of Christ's time were not averse to class warfare, themselves versus the Romans, and therefore yearned for a religious-military figure to save them, so some today want the church to be a quasi political-military force for the liberation of oppressed peoples.

A picture of a priest wearing a bullet belt in the form of a Cross dramatized this approach. This excessive version of liberation theology would raise the awareness of the oppressed to agree to class warfare and use the Gospel to justify armed revolt. Jesus was very clear that he had nothing to do with such behavior. His kingdom was not of this world and he would not raise the sword against anyone. He clearly wanted justice for all, but his strategy is that of the wounded healer. Only in the way of the cross is the victory over evil accomplished. The non-violent cross is the only answer he would ever give.

The seduction of violence enchanted the people of his time and it sometimes does the same today. The wish to use politics to solve what is essentially a spiritual problem existed then and exists now. The hunger to correct social evils with force was a perennial temptation for Christ's contemporaries. It has occurred again today. Jesus forbade it then. He does so now. Only the discipleship of the cross will work. This is the lesson he will teach insistently all during Passover Week.

Reflection

1. What has been my experience of and reaction to people in authority?
2. What kind of authority is most likely going to solicit my cooperation and obedience?
3. How would my faith lead me to obedience to the authority of God?
4. What was so striking about the way Jesus exercised his authority?
5. Why did the religious leaders ask Jesus by what authority he cleansed the temple?
6. Why did Christ's parable of the tenant vintners capture his audience's attention so quickly? What twist in the story did he add which shocked them?

7. How does Christ's teaching about rendering to Caesar and God appropriate responses affect my Christian civic responsibilities?
8. What lesson did I learn for my own life from Christ's teaching about marriage and resurrected life?
9. In a variety of ways, Jesus taught he was a spiritual not a political messiah. Who needs to hear that message today?
10. What do I think about the political uses of religion?

Prayer

Jesus, Lord and Master, your authority is full of love, honoring my freedom, but calling for an obedience that will make me fully human. Your commands are calls of love intending a creative remaking of my heart. Give me the wisdom to see the purpose of your commands and the grace to make an obedient response.

21 History's Future Is God's Secret

The end of the world grips and fascinates many people. Before the proliferation of nuclear bombs, it was thought that only God could terminate the world. Since the emergence of the superpowers and their nuclear arsenals, human beings now have the means to end the world.

One American warhead could flatten the Kremlin and buildings for two miles around it. The United States has 120 aimed at Moscow. If the Soviets launched a surprise attack of 3,000 warheads at the United States, between 70 million and 130 million Americans might be killed.

Ever since Jesus delivered his end of the world sermon, here heard in Luke's 21st chapter, solemn predictions about its arrival have accompanied natural and man-made catastrophes throughout history. Voices about earth's final days accompanied the Sack of Rome, the Black Plague, and the Holocaust and many other disasters.

Many associate the end of the world with a final cosmic battle, an "Armageddon," to be fought on the plains of Esdraelon in northern Palestine. The word *Armageddon* means "Mountain of Megiddo." This mountain overlooks the plains where the presumed conflict would be held. In biblical times this site was the scene for numerous critical battles. For the scriptural writer, it served as an image of a final conflict between the forces of good and evil.

Literal minded, alarmist Christian writers have speculated that the end of the world will begin with history's greatest military confrontation at Armageddon. They base their predictions on two major texts in the book of Revelation.

Chapter 9:13-19 describes what will happen when an angel blows the sixth trumpet. The horn's blast will signal the killing of two-thirds of the human race. This will be accomplished by the combined force of two hundred million soldiers along with plagues of fire, smoke, and sulphur. Chapter 16:12-16 amplifies this prediction by saying that when an angel pours out the sixth bowl of God's fury on the world, all the kings of the world will assemble for a cataclysmic battle. Where will this happen? "They then assembled the kings in the place that is called Armageddon" (Rv. 16:16).

By weaving these two texts together, these writers argue that when the angel blows the sixth trumpet calling the armies of the world to battle, another angel will disgorge the sixth bowl of God's fury. And all this will converge at the mountain of Megiddo, or Armageddon. The twentieth century's military technology has put new life into the primordial fears aroused by the sixth trumpet and the sixth bowl. A chilling addition to this anxiety was provided by the Persian Gulf war, with its threat of destruction by chemical, biological, and nuclear warheads. The fact that the war happened in lands associated with the texts of Revelation fed the literalist interpretations.

Those who espouse the literal readings of these texts argue that history's most awesome war at Armageddon signals the end of time. The proponents use prophetic passages in Daniel, Ezekiel, and Revelation to state that many nations — led by the Antichrist — will join Babylon (present day Iraq) in an invasion of Israel. But the Son of God will come and halt the slaughter. Some claim that this will usher in a thousand years of peace before the Last Judgement.

A careful meditation on Christ's actual sayings about the end of time radically tempers the above speculations.

Doomsday for the Temple and Jerusalem and the World (Lk. 21:1-24)

After praising a poor widow whose tiny offering surpassed the self congratulatory donations of the prosperous, Jesus addressed those whose awe of the temple's majesty obscured its future fate. He told them that this magnificent structure would be destroyed completely. He then went on to speak of the destruction of Jerusalem. He proceeded to use the twin devastations of temple and city as a master image of the end of the world itself, which event will be accompanied by the coming of the Son of Man.

The apostles asked him what signs would warn them that "these things" (destruction of temple, Jerusalem, world) were about to happen. Jesus told them there would be cosmic disasters: wars, earthquakes, famines, plagues, awesome sights in the skies, changes in the sun, moon and stars, whole nations disturbed by the roaring of the sea and its waves (see verses 9-11; 25).

Jesus warns them not be to be deceived by the destruction of the temple and the city. They should not conclude that these tragic events mean the end of the world is at hand. He then listed the long-term troubles mentioned above which will signal the end. Before any end of the world occurs, the disciples will suffer persecution from both political and religious powers just as Jesus did. Even close relatives will betray them for their faith commitment. Some will face martyrdom. In that hour they should not fear, for God will give them a wisdom to speak so eloquently that adversaries will be powerless to put them down. Physical death will not mean annihilation. In dying they will gain eternal life.

When meditating on the end of the temple, Jesus advised his followers to repel false messiahs and to act with deep faith in the face of persecution. Having shown how the destruction of the temple related to the world's end, he proceeded to do the same with the devastation of Jerusalem.

When Jerusalem faces its fate, they are to flee to the mountains. Life will become unbearable for those who remain. People will be killed, deported, and dispersed. The "time of the gentiles" has begun (see verse 24). This was not the beginning of the end of the world, but rather what the condition of the world would be like for those living in Christian history.

These words of Jesus have sustained the persecuted church from New Testament times to the present. The destruction of the temple and Jerusalem would have driven both Jews and Jewish Christians to deep depression. The loss of the Holy Place and the Holy City was bound to cause confusion and acute anxiety in the first Christians.

In the forty years between Christ's death and that catastrophe (70 A.D.), the beleaguered Christian communities could easily have wondered if the end of the world was upon them. Many of them had believed the second coming would happen anyway in their lifetime.

The sufferings they had already endured for their faith, the various martyrdoms — and now this end of the temple and the city — would seem to confirm that they would soon experience the final judgement.

Then the words of Jesus would come back to them. They should not be deceived, no matter how many tell them the "time has come." Persecution would continue after the destruction of the temple and city. The "time of the gentiles" had arrived. Simultaneously, the "time of Christian history" was only beginning.

Since then Christians have often experienced suffering because of their faith in Christ, whether in the Roman arenas or the Soviet gulags, be it Archbishop Becket at the hands of Henry II or Thomas More at the mercy of Henry VIII, or a Maximilian Kolbe in Auschwitz or an Isaac Jogues in Indian territory. The cross defines a Christian disciple.

Most Christians will not have to witness unto death itself, but they will have to practice faith and love within the often painful challenges of their families, communities, and work places. However demanding the cross may be, the words of Jesus remain. Lose the self. Take the cross. Follow Christ.

One need not indulge in fantasies about the timing of the world's end. There is work to be done now, a cross to be borne and a Gospel of love to be witnessed. There is a somberness about this aspect of Christianity, yet for those who live it, the experience is far more positive. It is the only way to grow in love. And that is the only way to acquire peace and joy.

The Second Coming (Lk. 21:25-38)

After laying out the immediate and long term vision of history, Jesus came to its final moment, the second coming of the Son of Man. He will confirm the judgement sinners have brought upon themselves by rejecting love. He will confirm salvation for those who have lived by love and welcomed it into their hearts.

In the hymn, "How Great Thou Art," judgement day is described in these words. "When Christ shall come, mid shouts of jubilation, to take me home, what joy shall fill my heart. And I shall bow in humble adoration, and there proclaim, 'My God, how great thou art.'"

The sentiments of this hymn set a positive tone for looking at the second coming and judgement day. This is different from the fire and brimstone approach so often preached for judgement day homilies in times past. As the needs of the faithful change, so do the ways of ministering to them. But exaggerations often result as well.

The one-sided judgement day of a fearsome God seems to yield to another kind of onesided-ness, the judgement day of the God of compassion. In their extreme form, neither approach allows accountability. The fearful approach seemed to allow no room for love and freedom of choice. A scary God bullied the soul into submission. The current love style seems to permit no room for sin, hence there is nothing to be accountable for. Hence one is either too frightened to be free enough to be accountable, or so laid back in the cocoon of affection that one does not imagine accountability is necessary.

Like all shifts in emphasis, something good is found and something valuable may be lost. Holding forth God's anger will make us think of sin, but may cause us to be uncertain about his forgiveness. Highlighting God's boundless affection for us will make us think of grace, but could also induce a sentimentality that deludes us into thinking we have no sins that need forgiveness.

Moreover, something curious has happened along the way. Just as the church moves the people to contemplate a kindly God of mercy, love, forgiveness, and compassion, the secular culture induces a fearful attitude toward the secular doomsday that threatens us. We hear of global warming, the greenhouse effect that will melt the polar icecaps and wash away one fourth of the earth. Others talk of a new ice age and worldwide destruction due to earthquakes, floods, and fire. This disaster-mania has its good side in that it makes us take seriously the need to avert environmental catastrophe by having a more responsible attitude toward guaranteeing clean air and clean water.

Yet on the lips of some, it sounds a little too desperate. In that case, the possible doom is not a cautionary tale for moral self renewal and social reform, but rather a helpless look at the loveless forces of nature.

Christ takes up the language of dissolution and crisis in a creative and positive way. If there is to be a crumbling of the old order that is but a giving way to a new order of love and hope. Jesus never talks like a wicked uncle who wants to scare the children. He wishes to brace his listeners for the rough seas ahead and equip them to face the trials that come from being a committed believer.

When Jesus speaks of the destruction of the temple and Jerusalem, he also speaks of the birth of the Christian community. When he talks about the actual end of the world and the second coming, he also points us to the birth of all believers in a new creation in eternity. His closing words in that section say no less. "But when these signs begin to happen, stand erect and raise your heads, for your redemption is at hand" (verse 28).

He urges us to have a spiritual alertness to be ready for our own personal end as well as the end of time. Our eternal destiny is too important to be forgotten in the drowsiness caused by carousing, drunkenness, and the anxieties of daily life. This need not be seen as a fear tactic on his part, but a genuine interest in our personal well being. Jesus is just as concerned about our quest for wholeness as we are, actually more so, since his attention to our well being does not flag, but ours often does. In the best sense of the word, Jesus is more interested in us than we are in ourselves.

At this point we are in a better position to see why the overly literal interpretations of the Armageddon writers do not fit the spirit of Christ's own vision of the future of history. Without a doubt, Jesus does use the colorful language of disaster imagery, which is echoed in the Book of Revelation in even more extensive and dramatic form. At no point does Jesus set dates, nor does the author of the Book of Revelation. In fact Jesus admonishes us to forget about dates. The future of history is God's secret. "But of that day and hour no one knows, neither the angels of heaven, nor the Son, but the Father alone" (Mt. 24:36). In fact Jesus emphasizes that it will come as a surprise (see verse 34).

Not only do we not know the date, we do not know the place either. Armageddon is a prophetic symbol not an exact prediction. Just as Babylon in the Book of Revelation is a code word for Rome, so also Armageddon is an image of the intense conflict that will accompany the world's end, however or wherever it will happen.

Humans always want to be in control, so it is not surprising that some people want to nail down the time and place of the world's end. Jesus says it is more important to concentrate one's energies on being a strong witness to faith, hope, and love. The best way to prepare for the end of the world is not to engage in vain speculations about the future, but to live today as though this were our last day on earth.

We should forget about controlling history and be more thoughtful about controlling impulses that negatively affect human dignity whether in ourselves or others. Control of history is a useless passion. Control of our passions is a useful goal.

Last, we should face the future with faith and forget trying to impose rational models on the flow of history. Followers of Marx tried to do that for most of the twentieth century and led all kinds of people into blind alleys. This does not mean we should not plan for the future. Wise planning makes sense so long as we also include surprise factors and are willing to be flexible in the face of changes in the forecasting. In religious terms, the wisest planning is always a faith act permitting the mystery of God to speak its own call to us. The future of history is God's secret.

Reflection

1. Why does the end of the world fascinate some people?
2. If Jesus told us the exact date when the world would end, what effect would that have on us?
3. Suppose northern Palestine were actually the Armageddon where the final conflict would be fought. What would that mean to me?
4. It is easy to see why the destruction of the temple and Jerusalem would depress Jews. Why would it disturb Christian converts from Judaism?
5. Why did Jesus use the destruction of the temple and Jerusalem as images of what would happen at the end of time?
6. If an angel appeared to me and told me the second coming would happen in five days, what would I do?
7. If I were asked to imagine what the second coming would be like, how would I do it?
8. What is the best Christian attitude toward the end of time and the second coming?

9. What would cause early Christians to think the end of the world and the second coming would happen in their lifetimes?
10. How do I handle news stories that report certain sects announcing exact dates for the end of the world?

Prayer

Lord Jesus, judge of the living and the dead, I know that you have come into my life in baptism and continue to come to me in the Eucharist and in my life of prayer with you. Remind me that my daily faith commitment and acts of love constitute the best way to prepare both for my own death as well as the end of the world and the second coming.

22 The Passion of Jesus Begins

The greatest of all meditations is the passion of Jesus Christ. Of all the words and acts of Jesus, none have the capacity to touch the heart with love and gratitude more than those that occurred during his passion. The story of the cross has converted hearts from sin to grace from apostolic times to the present. That is why the passion narratives are the longest and most moving parts of all four gospels.

Meditation on the passion will stir up feelings of thankfulness for what Jesus has done for us. That, of course will not be enough. Obedience to Jesus' teachings must accompany such feeling, otherwise our sentiments are a form of self-indulgence and a mockery of Christ's work. Just as truly, commitment to Jesus without any feeling for him is an imperfect form of relating to him.

As we turn to the passion we think about what Jesus said and did. We dwell on the various scenes of the Last Supper, the agony in the garden, the betrayal, scourging, crowning, carrying of the cross, and the crucifixion itself. We visualize these experiences of Jesus as real events, not just as vignettes written in a book. We will hear his words and those spoken to him. We see the injustices he endured and his forgiving reactions. We do not have to go up to heaven or fly to the farthest reaches of the seas. Jesus is as near to us as the gospel text which reveals him — indeed as near as our own heartbeat. We do this now in order to love and obey Jesus Christ.

Jesus Must Be Killed (Lk. 22:1-6)

Just before the events of Holy Week were to take place, Judas visited those priests who resolved that Jesus must be killed. In their eyes he had become a grave threat to their religious control of the people and an acute danger to their political relationships with the forces of occupation. His teachings disturbed them and upset their view of the sacred traditions of the covenant people. He was too popular for them to make a direct assault. Some other means must be found. They would find their solution in the discontent of Judas.

Judas had lost confidence in Jesus. He had never understood the profoundly spiritual nature of Christ's mission. Christ's powerful personality attracted him. He mistakenly thought Jesus would use his remarkable powers to mount a political rebellion. The other apostles also toyed with this political interpretation of Christ's messiaship. To some extent they could all be forgiven for this miscalculation since that vision of a messiah was sown deeply in the culture. Every child heard about a messiah who would be like their most beloved hero, the political-military genius and poet, David.

In a variety of ways, Jesus tried to disabuse the apostles of their false expectations. In their own clumsy ways, they did try to see what he was saying and they were loyal to him by their own standards. Only Judas had explicitly given up on him. As Luke says, "Satan entered into Judas" (verse 3). He went to the priests and colluded with them in a plan to betray Jesus into their hands. The story of the betrayal hung painfully over the Last Supper, an event meant to be a friendship meal and one that would become the Sacrament of Love, the Eucharist of the Lord.

Preparing for the Meal

The feast of the Passover and the Unleavened Bread was about to begin. The two major rituals associated with it originally came from ancient rural festivals. The ceremony of waving a sheaf of barley before the heavens and eating unleavened bread honored the spring barley harvest. The ritual of religiously sacrificing a new born lamb celebrated the birth of the spring lambs.

Originally these events were acts of gratitude to fertility gods. The Jewish people adapted them as sacred rituals to thank the one and true God for the fertility of the earth and their flocks, but above all in grateful memory of their (1) deliverance from the slavery of Egypt, (2) the gift of the covenant at Sinai and (3) the gift of the promised land. The rural rituals of the "bread and the lamb" acquired historical and theological meaning. Jesus as bread of life and lamb of

God would transform these rites into powerful forms of grace for every person in the world.

On Thursday of Passover Week, Jesus sent Peter and John to arrange for the Passover Meal. It would be held in an upper room. Most homes were one-story affairs, but some of them had a room on the roof, approached by an outdoor stairway. Often such rooms were used as attics for storage. Sometimes they were settings for meetings of rabbis with their disciples. Most likely this was the upper room for the last meal.

The apostles prepared for the supper by obtaining the unleavened bread and other foods for the table, along with a supply of wine. They also purchased a lamb and brought it to the temple for sacrifice. After the lamb was slain, the priest would pour out the lamb's blood on an altar, thereby giving God its life. A portion of the insides of the lamb would be burned on the altar, its smoke arising to God as another detail in the offering. After making a gift to the temple treasury, the apostles would bring the remainder of the lamb to the upper room for the supper. They would roast it on pomegranate wood on a fireplace outside the room.

Meanwhile all the participants in the meal would have bathed. (John's gospel adds the narrative of the washing of the feet.) The preparations for the Last Supper were complete.

The Great Supper

Jesus and the twelve assembled in the upper room and sat on floor cushions around the festival table. On that table they saw three freshly baked loaves of unleavened bread and a bowl of salt water to symbolize the tears of the Israelites during their slavery in Egypt. Salad bowls, filled with endive and seasoned with horseradish, recalled the bitterness of oppression. Dishes laden with an auburn colored mixture of apples, dates, and nuts, surrounded by cinnamon sticks summoned up images of the bricks their ancestors were compelled to make in the labor camps. Four cups of wine stood at each place setting. The roast lamb was the centerpiece. The meal began just after sundown, for in their reckoning the new day started at that time. The meal always had the solemnity of a religious service.

That evening Jesus seemed even more grave than ever as he said, "I have earnestly desired to eat this passover with you before I suffer" (verse 15). In these words, Jesus reached out to the apostles with an intimacy not so deeply expressed before. Jesus spoke of an "earnest desire" to celebrate this Passover with them before the trauma that lay ahead.

In telling them about his desire, Jesus was revealing the intensity of his love for them and for us. To grasp the full meaning of his desire, we should read Christ's words of affection in the Last Supper Discourse in John's gospel, chapters 13-17. Just as Jesus approached the Passover Meal that he would transform into the Eucharistic celebration with a frank expression of his feeling of affection for us and his will to love us, so should we bring the same attitudes to our participation in the Eucharist. Jesus began his First Eucharist with a declaration of love. From this we know how we should also begin our Eucharists.

The Words of Institution (Lk. 22: 17-20)

The words of the institution of the Eucharist are found four times in the New Testament, in the gospels of Matthew, Mark, and Luke and in Paul's first letter to the Corinthians, 11:23-26. By the time these words were recorded by the sacred writers, they had already been used many years in the liturgies of the primitive Christian communities, first by the apostles themselves and then by their successors. In reading the four versions of the words of institution, we will see small variations but note that the substance is identical in all four versions.

St. John's gospel gives us the longest account of what happened at the Last Supper, but does not record the words of institution. John gives us Christ's magnificent sermon on love at the Last Supper, in which Jesus explains the attitude and behavior commanded by participation in the Christian Passover/Eucharist. John provides us with Christ's explicit teaching on the meaning of Eucharist in the "Bread of Life" sermon in chapter 6.

At what moments in the Passover meal did Jesus speak the words of institution? Such a question was not on the minds of the sacred writers, hence they say nothing about it. Still, this does intrigue some of us today, and we may reasonably draw our own conclusion from what we generally know of the sequence of the rituals of a Passover meal.

The meal began with the blessing of the Unleavened Bread. Then it would be broken and distributed to the participants. During this time, someone would tell the story of Israel's deliverance from Egypt. Most likely this is where the first words of institution were spoken. After Jesus said the words of blessing, he broke with tradition, interrupted the usual ritual, and said the words of institution, "This is my body which will be given for you." He would suddenly have gained their absolute attention. He did something radically untraditional, introducing his remarkable saying into the meal so sacred that every word and movement was determined by custom and ritual. Not only did he speak new words, but a "word action" that transformed the bread into his body.

He told them they should not forget this, that they should do this "in memory of me." Given his extraordinary change of the ceremony that night, they certainly would never forget his command. Granting the fact he died in less than twenty four hours, they would surely remember his last words and commands at that supper. They would not completely appreciate or understand what he said and did. (Even now after 2,000 years of Eucharists, neither do we.) But in the regular celebrations of the Breaking of the Bread after Pentecost, they gradually came to appreciate how essential and central Eucharist was to their lives and that of the church.

What happened next? He would have raised the first of the four cups of wine at their place settings and offered a toast of gratitude to God for the exuberant love he had shown through all of sacred history and a toast of friendship among themselves, the apostolic community. Then the Supper of the Lamb began. During this section the celebrants drank the second cup of wine.

When the meal was finished, the host usually raised the third cup of wine and would say a prayer of thanks for the meal. They would follow this with a songfest, praising God in Psalms 115-118. In this moment where there is attention to the wine and the joy in one's heart, it seems that this was the moment Jesus chose to change the ritual again and introduce the words of institution over the wine. Luke expressly says it happened "after they had eaten." Jesus said, "This cup is the new covenant in my blood, which will be shed for you" (verse 20).

The gospels record no reactions from the apostles to these extraordinary changes in the Passover ritual. No questions about what Jesus meant. The mystery was too profound for discussions. Only when they did what Jesus commanded in the Breaking of the Bread after Pentecost, did they begin to sense the tremendous love and meaning contained in what Jesus had given them.

Betrayal, Ambition, and Denial (Lk. 22:21-38)

At all dinner parties the host and the hostess want to make sure all goes well. They want their guests to be relaxed and happy. They seat congenial people next to one another. They put soothing music on the soundtrack and try to be light and entertaining, hoping everyone will cooperate.

Jesus knew how to be pleasant enough. He must have been an attractive dinner guest, since he was invited to numerous banquets, as all the gospels attest. But at the Last Supper, Jesus exhibited his exact sense of realism. He would not settle for being an amusing host. For one thing, he realized what a daunting trial lay just ahead of him. Suffering and death intruded on what was normally a festive meal.

As a sound instructor, Jesus tried to prepare his apostles for the challenge to their loyalty and moral character that would begin within a few hours. First Jesus revealed to them that he knew one of them had already begun the process of betraying him. "The hand of the one who is to betray me is with me on the table" (verse 21). At the very moment the sacrament of love and commitment is instituted, there is a traitor at the table. By his words, Jesus gave Judas a chance to repent. He did not directly confront Judas with his sin. His indirect approach was meant to invite the poor man to convert before it was too late. This was a table of love. A traitor's hand was on that table. Love could only ache for a response of conversion. The apostles wondered who this could be. Luke describes Jesus letting the matter rest at that point.

The next jarring note was a quarrel among the apostles about who would be the top people among them in the kingdom. Jesus had set a tone of love at the meal. They can only think of power. Patiently Jesus teaches them one more time about humility and service as the outstanding traits of a kingdom person. The greatest should be the servant. They should not be like power people who get their pleasure by having other people wait on them.

Last came Christ's warning to Peter that he would deny him. Peter, feeling strong and protective of Jesus, declared that he would go to jail and die with him. Jesus told him that he would deny him three times before sunrise, greeted by the crowing of the cock. Peter crowed about his bravery like a cock. In the morning he would weep like a baby when he heard the rooster singing to the sunrise.

After a few more words of sage advice, Jesus raised the fourth cup of wine and led them in song. It is the only time we hear Jesus singing in the gospels. Like the thorn bird that sings only one song in its life, when it is about to die, Jesus lets his heart burst forth with melody just when incomparable sadness would overwhelm him.

Gethsemane —
Where They Crush the Grapes (Lk. 22:39-46)

Mount Zion and Mount Olivet are the "twin peaks" of the passion narratives. The temple crowned Mount Zion. Gethsemane crowned Mount Olivet. Jesus and the eleven (Judas had departed) left the upper room, descended Mount Zion, crossed the Brook Kedron and ascended Mount Olivet to the Garden of Gethsemane. Olive gardens carpeted the whole mountain. The prosperous owners, living in Jerusalem on Mount Zion, would use these walled gardens both as sources of income from the olive harvests and restful retreats from the noise and closeness of the city.

Jesus often used this garden retreat for nights of prayer. "But at night he would stay at the place called the Mount of Olives" (21:37). It "was his custom" (22:39). Tradition suggests that the garden belonged to Mark's family. The word *Gethsemane* means winepress. Just as the grapes were crushed in the winepress, so Jesus would be crushed that night by the thought of what he was to suffer. As the winepress squeezed the juices out of the grapes, the pressures of the forthcoming passion drew from Christ's body the tension of sweat "like drops of blood falling to the ground" (verse 44).

When they had arrived at the garden, Jesus told them to pray they would never have to be tested as heavily as he would be. Now he needed solitude. He could only face his decision alone. No one else could make it for him. Like any human being, he would have liked his support group to help him face his moment of truth. In fact he did want his apostles to pray with him. But he sighed and groaned knowing that he had to be totally alone now. His friends were not far away, simply a "stone's throw." But they might as well have been on the moon. Drowsy from the meal, they slept. Still blind and insensitive to the course of history, they frittered away their last moments with Jesus by snoring.

As the night enveloped Jesus, so the darkness raided his heart. He felt all the resistance to suffering and death that any human would. His basic survival instinct assailed his judgement and its passions tried to make him change his mind. He prayed what any human would pray, given so desolate a prospect. He asked his Father to take away the cup of suffering. Perhaps there is another way to save the world. Maybe sin and death can be overcome by some yet unexplored option. Jesus was perfectly capable of surveying any number of alternatives to what he knew he was called to do. This was his moment of truth.

Jesus had to bring himself to surrender to his Father's will at a moment when he felt unappreciated by those closest to him. He had a traitor and a denier among those he had trained the longest. The others were still hungry for worldly power. Even now, when he wanted them to pray with him, they thoughtlessly slept. And what about all the sinners of the world he came to save? Why bother going through with all this when they appreciated him so little?

This was the beginning of his last loneliness, one that was fought through silently here in the garden and one that would elicit from him a brutal shout of forsakenness on the cross (Mk. 16:34). He weathered his first storm of aloneness in the garden by his wondrous obedience and acceptance. "Not my will but yours be done" (verse 42). His last word on the cross in Luke's gospel will communicate the prayerful peace of his heart that his obedience obtained.

How Jesus Tried to Save Judas (Lk. 22:47-53)

Suddenly a crowd of soldiers noisily appeared in the garden. Judas led the group and walked up to Jesus and kissed him like a friend would. Jesus knew this was his last chance to save Judas. He looked at him with love and forgiveness and said words meant to invite him to repent even now despite the moral mess he had created for himself. Jesus asked him if he really wanted to betray him. Did he truly want to use a friendly kiss to undermine someone who felt nothing but forgiveness and compassion for him?

Jesus had struggled for the soul of Judas. He had one last opportunity, a deeply personal encounter, the context of one of humanity's most sacred gestures — a kiss — to touch somewhere deep in Judas' heart the wells of repentant response. Jesus was essentially a savior. He would not let natural resentment or the hurt feelings of a rejected lover impede his goal of cherishing the moral and spiritual future of Judas. Jesus would be nailed to a tree. He did not want Judas to hang from a tree in a fit of moral despair and graceless suicide.

This was one of a series of remarkably selfless gestures Jesus displayed throughout his passion. He continued to give love and hope even as he was being drowned by pain, hatred, and rejection. Tragically, Judas let this precious moment escape him. He was not open to love. He disappeared into the night of history, was last seen hanging from a tree, and then was buried in Haceldama, the field of blood.

The dazed disciples finally realized the doom that faced Jesus. They resorted to the only kind of power they would think of using in a violent situation, the power of the sword. One of them (John says it was Peter) cut off the ear of one of the high priest's servants. Jesus authoritatively shouted that they should stop the violence. He came to bring love and peace, to conquer the world by spiritual power, by soul force, not by the common brutalities that the world uses to solve its problems.

Again forgetting his own precarious state, Jesus calmly touched the servant's ear and healed him. Jesus never let the rush of history sweep him along. He is the prince of time. Let others push the course of events. Jesus will stop and heal an innocent servant. As soldiers around him stood with drawn swords (even one of his apostles),

Jesus momentarily slowed down the pace of events and witnessed what would be one of his greatest proposed gifts to the world, the gift of peace.

Then, digging deeper into the well of his own vast inner peace, he let silence descend on them while he looked at each burly guard and hostile priest. He asked them to feel the weapons in their hands, to see that he carried no knife, no club. He did not yell and scream in protest or shove away anyone who came near him. He rejected the posture of injured innocence. In the deep quiet of the garden, he asked them to notice the contrast. They came prepared to capture a robber. Instead they found a lamb.

Of course it was the lamb of God.

How Jesus Saved Peter (Lk. 22:54-65)

Jesus failed with Judas. He would win with Peter. The soldiers took Jesus to the house of the high priest where he would have his religious trial. The secular trial before Pilate would occur in the morning. Peter followed at a safe distance and then settled by a fire in the courtyard in front of the high priest's residence.

A woman took a close look at Peter and told everyone that Peter was a member of Christ's group. Peter protested that he did not know the man. A short while after that, someone else came up and identified Peter as "one of them," only to have Peter lie again about this. An hour later the accusation was repeated, adding this time that one could tell Peter was a Galilean by his accent and north-country behavior. (Judeans tended to think of Galileans as a step down in culture and religious fidelity.) Peter insisted he did not even know what the man was talking about.

Peter's denials proved that even a robust, generally courageous fighting man can be unnerved in a threatening situation. He was brave enough in the garden with ten other apostles whom he believed he could count on to brawl with him. He also felt he could lean on the powerful authority and presence of Jesus to back up his show of force. Here he sat alone by a fire amid hostile strangers, with a spread of Roman soldiers keeping guard in the public areas. His real and unvarnished affection for Jesus drew him to the scene, but the tenuousness of his situation as one man against the world cooled his bravado. He perhaps believed that in a tight situation like that, discretion is the better part of valor. What's a small lie after all, if one can live to fight another day? It might have been somewhat forgivable if he had not made such a show of force in the garden and of saying he would be a brave defender of Jesus.

After his third denial, the cock crowed. Just then Jesus was taken from the high priest's house. Jesus gave Peter a long and searching look. The Lord's eyes could not hide some look of reproach, but the greater message was a forgiveness meant to cause repentance in Peter. By this time one might think Jesus was driven by the indignities and injustice of the religious trial to be tempted to self pity or at least a somber form of introspection, but Jesus was determined to remain faithful to his call as savior, now above all in the acts of his passion.

Now it made more sense than ever to be an evangelist and reach out to touch hearts with forgiveness. Which is exactly what his penetrating look communicated to Peter. The very fact that Peter did not head for a rope and a tree like Judas tells the tale. Instead, Peter wept. His tears were healing. He received the gift of tears that led to his repentance and put him on the road to conversion. He would go on to lead the Christian community and become a martyr witness to Jesus in the city of Rome.

The Religious Trial (Lk. 22:66-71)

In this record of the religious trial, Jesus is asked two questions. Is he the Messiah? Is he the Son of God? On the issue of messiahship, Jesus replied that if he said he was they would not believe it. If he wanted to dialogue with them on the issue they would not speak. As to his being Son of God, he said to them, "You say that I am" (verse 70). He knew they had decided to eliminate him. Further discussion was useless.

His guards ridiculed him and beat him. The process of his passion had begun in earnest.

Reflection

1. What are examples of meals we have which possess religious like characteristic?
2. I have read the description of the upper room in the commentary. How did I picture it in my imagination before this?
3. If I put myself with the apostles at the Last Supper what might have gone through my mind when I heard the words of the institution of the Eucharist for the first time?
4. How have I reacted to those who have "betrayed" me? Would I be able now to treat a traitor with the forgiveness Jesus showed?
5. How would people today misuse religion for political purposes?
6. In what way would I deny Jesus like Peter did?
7. Have I had to make decisions alone in the solitude of my own heart? Discuss.
8. What occasions have I had where I "sweat bullets" in making a decision?
9. When I am having my own troubles, how could I overcome self pity and reach out to heal others?
10. How would I speak with Jesus when I meditate on his passion?

Prayer

Holy Shepherd and Lamb of God, you became more giving and loving the more you suffered. As the forces of pain closed in on you, trying to fill you with self absorption, you burst through with affection, healing, forgiveness, and love for each person you touched. Fill me with such a divine attitude that I may let your magnificent obsession with love pour through me to the world.

23 They Crucified My Lord

On Trial in Pilate's Court (Lk. 23:1-25)

On Friday morning Jesus was brought to Pilate at the Fortress Antonia. Normally, Pilate lived in a villa outside the city. Because of the potential for violence during Passover, he stayed in the city to keep his eye on troublemakers. Dramatic and artistic recreations of his city house and the space in front usually depict an imposing palace with a vast square in front.

The reality was more modest. The Antonia was a solid building, not overly large. The street in front was a typical narrow, winding one such as those found in all ancient cities. Hence the number of people who could pack into that assembly area was relatively small. The contingent of religious leaders, temple guards, and aroused supporters — at an early hour of the morning — would not exceed a few hundred people at the very most.

They met with Pilate at the door of his house, since it would be ritually unclean for them to enter the house of a gentile, especially on Passover. In their own court scene, they had condemned Jesus on religious grounds of presumed blasphemy. In front of Pilate's court, they changed the charges to secular, political ones. They falsely accused him of refusing to pay taxes to Caesar and of claiming to be a messiah-king.

In fact, Jesus had run away from the crowds that tried to make him king after his miracle of the bread. Second, he had explicitly taught that the taxes to Caesar should be paid, and publicly witnessed his own payment. The truth was that his lying accusers would love to mount a successful revolt against Caesar and never pay him another cent in taxes.

The charge about kingship caught Pilate's attention. Roman governors did not want local peoples striving for sovereignty. He questioned Jesus about his alleged kingship. Was he the King of the Jews? Jesus replied that Pilate was using words put in his mouth by the accusers. Luke has Pilate immediately declare Jesus innocent. No reasons are given for Pilate's conviction. That will be found in other gospels, especially in John. The accusers pressed their case, alleging that Jesus was another Galilean rebel. Pilate should know how many troublemakers have originated there.

When he heard that Jesus was a Galilean, Pilate sent him to Herod who was in charge of Galilee. Conveniently, Herod was in town for Passover. Herod had wanted to see Jesus because of his reputation as a miracle worker. Perhaps Jesus would perform some supernatural tricks for him in return for a deal that would release him from prison.

Herod tried in vain to make Jesus a house clown for the amusement of the court. He questioned him at length. At the same time, Christ's accusers kept up the pressure, noisily repeating the false charges. Jesus stood there in silence between an epicene king who had little to do but harass a helpless victim and a determined religious leadership whose burning ambition was to terminate our Lord. The silence of Jesus was its own form of reproach as it absorbed mockery from the throne and lies from the bystanders. In its own way, this was a form of evangelization, a depth outreach to Herod to stop and reflect. No words or arguments or miracles would convince Herod to convert. Only the sounds of silence provided the last opportunity to reach him. It did not work.

Impatient and frustrated, Herod had Jesus clothed in a resplendent robe (a not so private joke to underscore the "kingship" of Jesus) and sent him back to Pilate. The two of them finally became friends that day, united in their political, amoral pragmatism, dead souls that could not see a savior even when his great souled presence was before their eyes.

Pilate told the accusers that both he and Herod had investigated the case of Jesus Christ. There was no evidence that he deserved a conviction of a crime. The gospels show that Jesus had begun to influence Pilate who normally would have given little thought to the interests of a prisoner in the provinces. His ten-year public record as governor of Judea revealed a man who was amoral, pragmatic, and insensitive. The positive efforts he was making to save Jesus were out of character. Jesus had made some small headway in reaching the spiritual hunger and potential integrity that lay in Pilate — as in all human beings.

Even Pilate's ordering of the scourging of Jesus, perverse and brutal, was a means Pilate used to free Jesus. He hoped that the beating would be enough to satisfy the mob. The sight of a scourged man usually stirred human sympathy, but not in the case of Jesus. Last, Pilate thought of the Passover Amnesty, the Paschal Privilege in which one prisoner would be let go at Passover. He gave them a choice of Jesus the innocent one, or Barabbas the convicted murderer and rebel. The yelling crowd chose Barabbas and called for Christ's crucifixion. He yielded to them and gave them Barabbas.

Their hellish chants for the most cruel of deaths for Jesus increased in pitch. Pilate, who had shown some sign of a moral conscience, caved in. He had spent much of his life surviving by compromise and immoral decision making. It was not too late for him to change. The evil habits of a lifetime prevailed. History has memorialized his moral failure in the creed with the words, "suffered under Pontius Pilate." "He handed Jesus over to them to deal with as they wished" (verse 25).

Death March to Calvary (Lk. 23:26-31)

A soldier, carrying a sign, led the way of the cross. The sign bore the inscription that gave the reason for the execution, "Jesus Christ King of the Jews." It was written in three languages, Latin for the international rulers, Greek for the international culture, Hebrew for the local people. A trumpeter sounded the horn to advise people to stay out of the way, but also to invite last minute witnesses who might come forth and bring new evidence to save the prisoner. If they came, a trial was held on the spot, which if it proved the prisoner's innocence, meant he could go free.

Jesus came next, carrying the cross bar. The vertical post was already at Calvary, meaning skull hill, probably because many beheadings were also held there. Some soldiers accompanied the march to make sure no one interfered with the progress. After a time, Jesus must have appeared too weak to carry his cross all the way to the mound of execution, so the soldiers drafted Simon of Cyrene to carry it for him the remainder of the journey.

While all his apostles, save John, ran away in fright, many good people remained faithful to Jesus, especially a group of mourning women who attempted to comfort him and give him moral support. A later tradition claims that one of them, Veronica, took a cool towel and gently soothed his face with it. The tradition adds that her towel received the miraculous imprint of Christ's face. Jesus was grateful and appreciated their loyalty and kindness, but in the full spirit of his whole passion, he comforted them instead.

He reminded them that they would also suffer for the sake of his name. They must save their tears for their children and families who would suffer persecution for their faith in him. Things will become so bad for the new Christian community that its members will ask the mountains to fall on them. What is being done to him, "the green wood," will be painfully imposed on the persecuted church, "the dry wood."

Two others, both criminals, were part of the death march that day.

They Nailed Him to the Wood (Lk. 23:33-43)

The gospels do not describe the process of crucifixion. Other sources do that for us, noting that some victims were tied to the crosses and others nailed. We know that Jesus was nailed to the cross from the testimony of Christ's words to Thomas after the resurrection, when Jesus wants to strengthen his faith. He asks Thomas to put his hands in the scars left by the nail marks (Jn. 20:25,27).

The nails were driven into the are just behind the wrist bone. Had they been dug into the palms, the hands could not be held by them as the body weight pulled away. Nails were also driven into his feet. Very likely there was a foot rest as well as a small post for "sitting" so that the body could last longer on the cross. Death came by gradual asphyxiation usually after a week of suffering.

John's gospel points out that Jesus died very quickly, probably because the scourging was too severe and the other beatings had already driven most of the life out of him. The criminals had their legs broken so they would die quickly, both because of the shock of the beating and their inability to lift themselves up to breathe. Jewish laws did not allow bodies to be exposed like that on the sabbath, so a quicker death was required.

The mound at Calvary was a small, elevated section of packed earth. The vertical post was therefore not very far removed from the onlookers. So close was Jesus both to his family and his detractors that he could hear them very well and look almost directly into their eyes.

Crucifixions were intimate events. Hence when various groups — soldiers, religious rulers, bystanders from the mob at the Antonia — began yelling at him and taunting him to save himself, Jesus could hear them clearly and look at each one of them. Their malice went unabated even when they had won their "victory." In his weakened condition, the natural juices of resentment could surface readily and, in any other man, not be restrained by this unfair and gratuitous psychological punishment.

Yet, though he was experiencing their undiluted malice, Jesus singled them out for his first word from the cross. He had come to offer them forgiveness for their sins. They were the lost ones he came to save. As he gazed at them, he wanted to make them the first beneficiaries of his saving cross. "Father, forgive them, they know not what they do" (verse 34).

Luke then draws out attention to the criminals crucified with Jesus. Their story is well known. One of them, despairing in the face of imminent death, caught the spirit of Christ's detractors and joined in cursing him out. The other one came to Christ's defense, and in a courageous and kindly way tried to argue his fellow sufferer to face the facts. They were actual criminals. They deserved what they were getting.

He pleaded Christ's innocence both with the other criminal as well as in front of the onlookers. At last a witness came forward to speak the truth about Jesus in the most unlikely of courtrooms, during the death watch at Calvary. What joy must have flooded the heart of Jesus in this dark hour. Here was a certified sinner defending the savior.

What might have touched this good criminal who had so little contact with Jesus? Christian imagination has suggested that he was housed with Jesus in the detention cell during that final night. In those hours of silence next to the Son of God, preparing for death, the man was profoundly affected by the witness of Jesus. Then, minute by minute, he would have seen the way Jesus reacted to the mob and Pilate, the scourging (the criminals were also scourged) and the disappointing choice of Barabbas.

This man could tell that Jesus was not just an unjustly treated good man. There was a depth of spirituality about him that reached his own heart. He had come to believe Jesus was the savior. That is why he said, "Jesus, remember me when you come into your kingdom" (verse 42). Jesus joyfully welcomed this lost one with his absolute assurance. "Today, you will be with me in Paradise" (verse 43).

Christ's Night Prayer and Death (Lk. 23:44-49)

Each gospel recalls one or another "prodigy" that accompanied the dying of Jesus. Luke records the darkness that covered the earth from noon onward. He also notes the tearing of the veil of the temple. These mysterious echoes of the singular event at Calvary frame Christ's final words from the cross, "Father, into your hands I commend my spirit" (verse 46).

The traditional devotion of the Seven Last Words puts this saying of Jesus last, even though John's gospel's last word of Jesus is, "It is finished" (Jn. 19:30). John's ending is a liturgical declaration in which Jesus the high priest concludes his act of obedient worship and service. Luke's conclusion is a devotional ending, a uniquely personal way of finishing the death scene. Jesus had learned these words as a night prayer from his mother, Mary, in his childhood, like all the children in his village.

Luke underlines the fact that Jesus delivered this deeply moving prayer in a "loud voice." Jesus is thus in command of his destiny to the end. He did not drift away in a dreamy haze, done in by the forces of death. Jesus was always a magnificently centered and purposeful person. As the Word made Flesh, he could not be otherwise. His last breath already signaled the victory over death that would be the first result of his life and passion.

At his death, the veil of the temple was torn apart. It symbolically hid the presence of God who lived mysteriously in the thick darkness. By the coincidence of the opening of the veil and the death of Jesus, the prodigy was meant to say that Christ's death was a revelation of God. The first one to notice this was the special soldier guarding the body of Jesus.

The impact of the divine presence at that site, the beginning of the return of the Word made Flesh to heavenly glory, broke through and invited the man to faith. He was ready and gloriously open. The first convert caused by the redeeming death of Jesus was a Roman soldier. Overwhelmed, he glorified God and exclaimed in faith, "This man was innocent beyond all doubt" (verse 47). In Mark's gospel he says, "Truly this man was the Son of God" (Mk. 16:39).

Burial: The Grain of Wheat Is Sown
in the Ground (Lk. 23:50-56)

Out of the blue came forth Joseph, a member of the religious council, though he did not consent to their action against Jesus. He came from Arimathea, also called the village of Rama, remembered for a slaughter of children that took place there. Every mother who subsequently lost a child through violence remembered Rachel of Rama mourning and loudly wailing her dead children. Now a man whose birthplace was best identified for mourning comes forth to arrange the burial of Jesus. He gave him his newly built tomb that was near the place of execution.

Joseph went to Pilate and asked for Christ's body. He helped remove the body from the cross, a scene that is immortalized in Michelangelo's pieta. Christian devotion has always imagined Jesus being laid in the arms of Mary before being taken to the tomb. But they had to hurry because the bodied must be in the grave before sundown. The Galilean women who had followed Jesus and comforted Mary watched the burial. Then they went home to prepare spices and perfumed oil which they would use for an extensive anointing of the body on Sunday.

"Then they rested on the sabbath according to the commandment" (verse 56).

Reflection

1. If I were asked to explain why a political opportunist like Pilate made several efforts to save Jesus, what would I say?
2. How can one say that Christ's silence before Herod was an effort to reach the heart of this man?
3. What happens to otherwise religious people that would make them scream for the death of an innocent man and ask for the release of Barabbas?
4. Why did Pilate think the scourging of Jesus would motivate his accusers to relent and let him go?
5. In meditating on Simon of Cyrene, what comes to my mind?
6. What do I learn from Christ's beautiful words to the comforting women who walked with him on the way of the cross?
7. How could I develop the capacity for forgiveness that Jesus displayed in the face of his tormentors?
8. What elements brought about the conversion of the good criminal at Calvary?
9. How would I imagine the feelings of the soldier at the cross who was converted at the death of Jesus?
10. In imagination, gaze on the pieta and express what Mary would be experiencing.

Prayer

Lord Jesus, crucified God, the story of your dying remains the most powerful and heart converting of all meditations. Bring me again and again to the cross where I may experience your saving graces. May your cross continue to change my values and attitudes into those that you witnessed so powerfully at Calvary. I rest in your love.

24 The Green Blade Rises from the Buried Grain

Christ Our Lord Is Risen Today (Lk. 24:1-12)

At dawn on the third day, Sunday morning, the women came to the tomb with their spices and perfumed oil to anoint the body of Jesus. There had not been enough time to complete these burial rites on Friday afternoon. The burial chamber was a small room hollowed out of rock. Spaces were carved out along the walls. Here the bodies were laid to rest. The body would first be laid on a polished stone slab on the floor at the center of the chamber. Here the anointing would take place. In the Church of the Holy Sepulchre in Jerusalem, such a stone of anointing is preserved, tradition maintaining it was the one used in Christ's burial.

The door of the tomb was a heavy circular stone which could be rolled away when one wished to enter the area. The women were surprised to see that the stone door had been moved and the entrance was open. They were even more amazed when they saw that the body of Jesus was gone. At that moment two men in radiant garments appeared to them. Terrified by these angel like figures, the women fell to the ground and touched their heads to the earth. These heavenly messengers announced the resurrection of Jesus. "Why do you seek the living among the dead? He is not here, but he has been raised" (verse 6). The angels reminded the women about the times that Jesus had foretold both his crucifixion and resurrection.

The women recalled Christ's words, but also remembered that they had not understood them. In their minds, like all the others, they practiced denial about Christ's prediction of his violent end. They just did not accept that. And, as to resurrection, what could that mean? The only person that was expected to come back again was Elijah, and that was because he had not died a proper death, but had been taken alive in a fiery chariot into the skies. As they stared in amazement at the empty tomb, they now realized what Jesus had meant. The heavenly visitors had clarified that for them.

Who were these Easter women? Luke says they were Mary Magdalene, Joanna, and Mary, the mother of James. There were others as well, but Luke does not name them. These women, with Mary Magdalene at their head, returned from the tomb and announced the resurrection of Jesus to the eleven apostles. The apostles did not believe them and considered that their message was nonsense.

Peter, however, did feel himself disposed to their incredible story. He went to see the tomb for himself. He found the empty tomb. The body was gone. Only the burial shroud remained. Luke says he was "amazed." This experience of radical wonder in Peter was a prelude to his faith in the resurrection. Human wonder is the human precondition for faith, because it disposes the person to be open to mystery, both human and divine.

The gospels frequently note how the miracles and teachings of Jesus caused wonder in people. They also show us a Jesus who keeps pulling everyone beyond wonder to faith. It is not enough to stand before a miracle with one's mouth open. The day must come when the heart has to be open as well. Mary Magdalene and the women have already made their Easter act of faith. They believe Jesus has truly risen. The next step was to bring the apostles to faith. The splendid story of Emmaus describes the turning point in this process.

The Emmaus Seven-Step Conversion Program (Lk. 24:13-35)

Emmaus means "warm wells." The meaning suits well the warmth of this story which is one of the most beloved in all of Scripture. The village of the warm wells was seven miles from Jerusalem. On Easter Sunday evening two disciples embarked on this seven mile walk to Emmaus. One of them was named Cleopas. The name of the other remains unknown. Christian imagination has supplied numerous possibilities, one of which seems as reasonable as any — the man's wife, Mrs. Cleopas.

This masterful narrative has attracted the attention of countless commentators because its developmental quality applies so well to various ways of perceiving Christian spiritual growth. Father James Dunning has drawn from the narrative an ingenious set of seven steps in the evolution of the awareness of the two disciples, from despair over Christ's death to faith in his resurrection. We will follow his seven steps and adapt them with our own observations. The essence of the story is how Christ evoked from the disciples faith in his resurrection. The master teacher patiently led them from hopelessness to celebration. This is how he did it.

1. Let There Be Stories.

Jesus finds the two disciples walking along the road, deep in solemn and grave discussion. They do not recognize him because they will need faith to do that. Only faith is able to perceive the risen Christ. One thing is clear in all the resurrection narratives, namely, that there was widespread disbelief and doubt about Christ's resurrection among the very people one would expect to have it. This is clear from the numerous non-recognition stories in all the gospels. It was precisely the ministry of the Risen Jesus to call and lead people to faith in his risen reality. This Emmaus story is an excellent example of how he did it. It is also a superb model for our own journey to deeper faith, as well as a way to help others make the same journey.

Jesus joined these two depressed people and asked them why their faces were so downcast. In other words, he encouraged them to tell their stories. He gave them permission to talk about their anxieties and sorrows. He did not approach them as one ready to solve their problems or answer their questions. They needed the gift of attitudinal change, not a religion lesson at this point. That would come in time when they were ready.

Instead, Jesus gave them that reassuring affection that let them grieve and mourn by expressing the sources of their pain. They were in a dark tunnel. Jesus was inviting them to come out of it and into the light. Once they were in the light, they would begin to see the truth. Trapped by their grief, they would see nothing. In receiving from him the freedom to tell their stories, they would inch their way out of the tunnel and take the first step to conversion and faith. This was the first gift Jesus gave them.

2. Let There Be Questions.

Next they besieged Jesus with questions. Where has he been the last couple of days? Doesn't he know what happened to Jesus of Nazareth? Can he possibly have not heard of the tragedy of the crucifixion? Could he have missed the rumors brought by the women that he was alive? How could anyone believe that? Jesus kept their questions coming. He did not interrupt them with answers. Nor did he insist they deal with his questions. Just as he listened with empathy to their stories, he also heard with interest the flow of questions surging from their hearts.

He taught us here an old truth. Just because a person asks us a question does not mean they want us to give them an answer. Sometimes they just want sympathy and understanding, not solutions to their problems from us. Obviously there is a distinction in questions here. We are not referring to simple information questions such as what is the time of day, or which way to the nearest post office. The questions talked about here are those that deal with people's deeper personal concerns and problems, or perhaps even their philosophical and religious inquiries. We should allow them to keep asking their questions, refining them, framing them in clearer terms till the question's final form begins itself to reveal the answer. Jesus treated the Emmaus disciples that way and it did them a world of good.

3. Let There Be Community.

During his Galilean ministry, Jesus had taught that where there are two or three gathered in his name, he would be present to them. Cleopas and his companion were gathered in Christ's name. They could think and talk of nothing else but Jesus and what happened to him. Lovingly linked in Christ's name, they were given the extraordinary privilege of having Jesus come into their presence, not just spiritually as in our case, but physically.

Jesus came to them to form them into a living, personal friendship and community with him. As he walked and talked with them, he was fast becoming their friend and the three of them were experiencing a bond of love growing by the hour. He would build the bonds of friendship before forging the bonds of doctrine. For certain intellectuals it might be that an abstract presentation of the truth is their road to love.

For most of the human race, it is love that is the door to truth. First people fall in love and then they want to know the truth about one another. The sequence in religion follows this tried and true path of human nature. The grace of Jesus built upon the nature of the disciples. Jesus created a warm little community with his friends. Only then was he ready to share his vision of the Scriptures with them. Only then were they ready to hear it.

4. Let There Be Tradition.

Jesus had led them out of the tunnel of their grief and gloom by listening to their stories with empathy. He brought them further into the light by encouraging them to get all their questions on the table to the point where these had been sifted clean and had begun to suggest their own answers. He worked on his relationship with them until they felt at home with him and trusted him. Here was someone they could listen to and love.

They had become intimate enough that Jesus could venture a mild reproach about their foolishness, being so slow to believe what the prophets had taught. He then proceeded to give them a lesson in Scripture. He took the Torah, the prophets, and the wisdom writers and showed how Jesus fulfilled what they were all talking about. We can only envy them hearing the greatest master of Scripture who ever lived giving them a personal, customized vision of the meaning of the Scriptures.

What did he say? Did he take the Genesis story of the woman whose offspring would crush the serpent and say, "Well that was Mary, the mother of Jesus." Did he take Isaiah 53 and show how Jesus lived out the substance of that prophecy in his passion and death? Did he take Ezekiel 37 where a valley of soldiers' bones are given new life by God's breath and tell them that the real fulfillment of that lay ahead at Pentecost when the Holy Spirit will breathe divine life into the 120 people in the upper room? We shall never know.

The lesson for us is that the sharing of our faith is a necessary part of helping others to grow in the faith they already have. Or to help people come to faith for the first time. We never forget that the Holy Spirit is the author and sustainer of faith, but the Spirit normally works through human channels.

5. Let There Be Religious Experience.

The disciples noticed that something was happening to them. They felt something changing and transforming them. Their hearts which had been heavy with hopelessness now felt light. More than that, their hearts were burning with joy. They were having a religious experience. They felt the closeness of a presence which they knew to be divine. They did not know it yet, but the Jesus who walked with them was the Eternal Word who had emptied himself of glory and was now moving with divine intensity again to the fullness of glory.

It must be admitted that a statement like this is an attempt to grasp a deep mystery. No journey image can be applied to the return of the Eternal Word to glory in quite the same way we would apply a forward movement in our physical order. Still the dynamism of the return of the Word to glory was happening somehow and the effect was being felt in those two fortunate disciples. One thing was certain. They had felt miserable. Now they felt transfixed with joy.

The lesson of this step in the faith journey is that we need an experience of the divine presence. Jesus had already given them a warm human experience by forming a community with them and inspiring them with his Scripture lesson. Now Jesus carries them further and fills their hearts with a warm divine experience. Love will settle for nothing less than the absolute and the utterly transcendent. Jesus made sure his friends had that privilege.

Cleopas and his companion said it best themselves. "Were not our hearts burning within us?" (verse 32).

6. Let There Be Celebration.

They finally arrived at the village of the Warm Springs. They were so captivated with their "new friend" that they insisted he stay with them for dinner. Dining together is one of our most intimate forms of sharing. They felt so close to him they did not want to let him go. They needed to celebrate the change that had come over them and to do it with the one who caused it. Their faith was almost ready to burst forth into visibility and the beginnings of maturity. If they had a revelation, they would be ready to respond.

This is exactly what happened during the meal. A point was reached, just as in the Last Supper, when Jesus departed from the normal ritual flow of a pleasant dinner and broke bread and blessed wine in such a way that Cleopas and his friend experienced a revelation. They recognized that their companion was Jesus Christ risen from the dead. Here, the sacramental encounter led immediately to a personal, visible encounter with Jesus.

The Lord, however, immediately vanished from their sight. They held in their hands the bread become his Body and the cup of wine become his Blood. They must live with faith. In the sacrament they would encounter the Risen Christ. Hence their "Breaking of the Bread" was a dual celebration, first of a process that brought them from despair to grace; second, of the reception of the gift of faith that would sustain them the rest of their lives.

7. Let There Be Mission.

Enthusiasm flooded their whole being. Despite the late hour they set out and walked the seven miles back to Jerusalem to share their good news. The best way to keep one's faith is to share it with another. The surest method for developing in faith is to give others the opportunity to believe. Evangelization is a sign of a dynamic church. It is the evidence of dynamic members.

The converted disciples understood that they must share their good news with the apostles. Their happiness was too much to keep to themselves. They now had the inner drive that would make them missionaries. As it turned out the apostles also were overflowing with joy for they too had arrived at faith in the Risen Jesus.

The full cycle of the Gospel was completed, only to be started again countless numbers of times to our own day. Each of us will have our own Emmaus walk to make. Jesus will take us through the seven stages. In the power of the Spirit, we will take others through those steps until the plenitude of the kingdom is reached in God's good time.

Easter Appearances in Jerusalem (Lk. 24:36-53)

As the excited Emmaus disciples, the eleven apostles and others shared their glorious experiences of the risen Christ, the Lord himself came into their midst. The awed assembly fell silent and heard the first words of the resurrected Jesus. "Peace be with you" (verse 36). In Scripture all heavenly manifestations begin with the gift of peace and the dispelling of fear. Heaven seeks union and reconciliation with earth. God loves us and does not want to frighten us.

The whole point of Christ's saving work was to bring peace and reconciliation to each human heart. At his birth the angels sang of him as a Prince of Peace. At his resurrection, his very first word is "Peace." Jesus continued with his ministry of rounding out the training in faith his followers needed. He was truly the same Jesus whom they knew in Galilee.

Though glorified now, Jesus has not lost his humanity. He took their hands and urged them to touch him, hug him, and feel his bones and flesh. While he now manifests his glory as Word, he still is the Word made flesh. Even though they now believed, it still required firming up and strengthening. Easter faith needed a growth process. Jesus went further and told them he would like something to eat, to emphasize even more the reality of his humanity. He was no ghost.

Then he gave them a Scripture lesson much in the same vein as he did with the Emmaus disciples. Now he adds words about their duty to evangelize peoples. They should preach repentance and forgiveness of sins to all nations. They should go forth as missionaries of peace, providing their listeners with the experience of their own forgiving and loving attitude, witnessing Christ's way of dealing with them. This way, forgiveness becomes the condition of repentance. The sequence of salvation thus has a circular motion. Forgiveness is the condition of repentance, which in turn, when expressed, obtains forgiveness.

There would be one more major step before they were ready to evangelize. Jesus would send them the gift of the Holy Spirit who would teach them the full meaning of the Gospel message and penetrate their whole being with graces to make them powerful witnesses to Christ everywhere. How this occurred is described in Luke's next book, The Acts of the Apostles.

Luke ends his gospel with a brief description of the Ascension of Jesus into heaven. Meanwhile the men and women who awaited the coming of the Spirit spent their days at the temple with great joy praising God. Luke's prayerful gospel opened at the temple and closes there.

With these thoughts, St. Luke concludes his gospel.

Reflection

1. As I read of how the apostles did not at first believe in the resurrection, what does that say to me about what my reaction might have been?
2. Jesus encouraged the Emmaus disciples to tell their stories. Why did he do that?
3. Why is it important to draw out people's questions and not rush in too quickly with answers?
4. Why did Jesus build the bonds of friendship before getting to the bonds of doctrine?
5. If I were reconstructing what I thought Jesus gave in his Emmaus Scripture lesson, what would I produce?
6. If I never had a religious experience of Jesus, what would that do to my relationship with him?
7. Why is faith a necessary virtue when facing the truth of the resurrection of Jesus?
8. How does the study of Scripture enable me to have a greater missionary spirit?
9. Why did Jesus keep stressing he was really human after the resurrection?
10. Why do I need the Holy Spirit for my daily Christian life and for my missionary efforts?

Prayer

Risen Jesus, I hear your first risen word, Peace. I am grateful for this most needed gift of peace. You reconcile me to you, to others, and to myself. As your peace takes more and more possession of me, I will be able to bring that to others. I praise you forever.